God loves you just the way you are,
but he refuses to leave you that way.
He wants you to be . . .

JUST LIKE JESUS

MAX LUCADO

This Billy Graham Evangelistic Association special
edition is published with permission from Word
Publishing, a division of Thomas Nelson, Inc.

WORD PUBLISHING

NASHVILLE

A Thomas Nelson Company

Unless otherwise indicated, Scripture quotations used in this book are from the Holy Bible, New
Century Version, copyright © 1987, 1988, 1991 by Word Publishing, Dallas, Texas 75234. Used
by permission.

Other Scripture references are from the following sources:

The Holy Bible, New International Version (NIV). Copyright © 1973, 1978, 1984, International
Bible Society. Used by permission of Zondervan Bible Publishers.

The King James Version of the Bible (KJV).

The Living Bible (TLB), copyright © 1971 by Tyndale House Publishers, Wheaton, Ill. Used
by permission.

The Message (MSG), copyright © 1993. Used by permission of NavPress Publishing Group.

The New King James Version (NKJV), copyright © 1979, 1980, 1982, 1992, Thomas Nelson,
Inc., Publisher.

J. B. Phillips: The New Testament in Modern English, Revised Edition (PHILLIPS). Copyright ©
J. B. Phillips 1958, 1960, 1972. Used by permission of Macmillan Publishing Co., Inc.

New American Standard Bible (NASB), © 1960, 1977 by the Lockman Foundation.

The Revised Standard Version of the Bible (RSV). Copyright © 1946, 1952, 1971, 1973 by the
Division of Christian Education of the National Council of the Churches of Christ in the USA.
Used by permission.

The Jerusalem Bible (TJB). Copyright © 1968 by Darton, Longman, & Todd, Ltd., and Doubleday
& Co., Inc.

The New Revised Standard Version Bible (NRSV), © 1989 by the Division of Christian Education of the National Council of the Churches of Christ in the USA.

The Good News Bible: The Bible in Today's English Version (TEV) © 1976 by the American
Bible Society.

Library of Congress Cataloging-in-Publication Data

Lucado, Max.
    Just like Jesus : living in the heart of the Savior / by Max Lucado.
      p. cm.
    Includes bibliographical references.
    Previously ISBN 0-8499-1296-2 (hardcover). — ISBN 0-8499-6285-4 (audio)
    1. Jesus Christ—Example. 2. Spiritual life—Christianity. I. Title.

    ISBN 0-913367-34-6

Cover design by T. M. Williams
Cover photo by Patrick Cone

To the staff of Oak Hills Church of Christ

---

*God is fair; he will not forget
the work you did and the love you showed
for him by helping his people.*

HEBREWS 6:10

CONTENTS

———————— ✦⤸✦⤛✦ ————————

My writing room is different. Just a few months ago these walls were white. Now they are green. Once these windows were curtain covered; today they are shielded by shutters. My chair used to sit on a tan carpet, but the tan has been replaced by white. To be candid, I had no problem with the tan carpet. It looked fine to me. Nor did I object to the white walls and curtains. From my perspective the room looked fine.

But not from my wife's perspective. Denalyn loves to decorate. Better stated, she *has* to decorate. She can no more leave a house unchanged than an artist can leave a canvas untouched or a musician a song unsung.

Fortunately she limits her remodeling to what we own. She's never shuffled the furniture in a hotel room or reorganized pictures in the houses of friends. (Though she has been tempted.) She only remodels what we possess. But mark it down: what we possess will be remodeled. For Denalyn, it's not enough to own a house; she has to change the house.

As for me, I'm content with owning the house. My tastes are, shall we say, less sophisticated. In my view a chair and a refrigerator go a long way toward award-winning interior design. For me the herculean task is purchasing the house. Once the transaction is complete and the house is bought, I'm ready to move in and rest.

Not so with Denalyn. As the ink is drying on the deed, she is moving in and remodeling. I wonder if she inherited this trait from her Father, her heavenly Father. You see, the way Denalyn views a house is the way God views a life.

God loves to decorate. God *has* to decorate. Let him live long enough in a heart, and that heart will begin to change. Portraits of hurt will be replaced by landscapes of grace. Walls of anger will be demolished and shaky foundations restored. God can no more leave a life unchanged than a mother can leave her child's tear untouched.

It's not enough for him to own you; he wants to change you. Where you and I might be satisfied with a recliner and refrigerator, he refuses to settle for any dwelling short of a palace. After all, this is his house. No expense is spared. No corners are cut. "Oh, the utter extravagance of his work in us who trust him" (Eph. 1:19 MSG).

This might explain some of the discomfort in your life. Remodeling of the heart is not always pleasant. We don't object when the Carpenter adds a few shelves, but he's been known to gut the entire west wing. He has such high aspirations for you. God envisions a complete restoration. He won't stop until he is finished. And he won't be finished until we have been shaped "along the . . . lines . . . of his Son" (Rom. 8:29 MSG).

Your Creator is remaking you into the image of Christ. He

wants you to be just like Jesus. This is the desire of God and the theme of this book.

Before we go any further, may I stop and say thank you? To spend these moments with you is a high privilege, and I want you to know how grateful I am for the opportunity. My prayer for all who read these words is simple. May God open your eyes so that you can see Jesus. And in seeing Jesus, may you see what you are called to be.

I also would like to introduce you to some of the folks who made this book possible. Here is a salute to some dear friends:

To Liz Heaney and Karen Hill—Few editors cut and paste with such skill and kindness. Thanks again for another valiant work.

To Steve and Cheryl Green—Just having you near simplifies my world. Thank you for all you do.

To the wonderful family of Christians at Oak Hills—Though your taste in a senior minister may be questionable, your love for this one is appreciated. Here is to a decade of work together. May God grant us many more.

To Scott Simpson—What a clutch shot! The timing was perfect for us both. Thanks for the inspiration.

To the skilled team at Word Publishing—Through times of transition, you are reliable and true. I'm honored to be on your roster.

To my daughters Jenna, Andrea, and Sara—If heaven is missing three angels, I know where to find them.

To Kathy, Karl, and Kelly Jordan—The birth of this book coincided with the passing of your husband and father, Kip. He is sorely missed. On the crowded canvas of publishing, his figure rose high above the others. He will never be replaced, and he will always be remembered.

And most of all, to Denalyn—What you've done to our house is nothing compared to what you've done in my heart. Decorate all you want, honey.

———— ❧✦❧ ————

A HEART LIKE HIS

What if, for one day, Jesus were to become you?

What if, for twenty-four hours, Jesus wakes up in your bed, walks in your shoes, lives in your house, assumes your schedule? Your boss becomes his boss, your mother becomes his mother, your pains become his pains? With one exception, nothing about your life changes. Your health doesn't change. Your circumstances don't change. Your schedule isn't altered. Your problems aren't solved. Only one change occurs.

What if, for one day and one night, Jesus lives your life with his heart? Your heart gets the day off, and your life is led by the heart of Christ. His priorities govern your actions. His passions drive your decisions. His love directs your behavior.

What would you be like? Would people notice a change? Your family—would they see something new? Your coworkers—would they sense a difference? What about the less fortunate?

————

Would you treat them the same? And your friends? Would they detect more joy? How about your enemies? Would they receive more mercy from Christ's heart than from yours?

And you? How would you feel? What alterations would this transplant have on your stress level? Your mood swings? Your temper? Would you sleep better? Would you see sunsets differently? Death differently? Taxes differently? Any chance you'd need fewer aspirin or sedatives? How about your reaction to traffic delays? (Ouch, that touched a nerve.) Would you still dread what you are dreading? Better yet, would you still do what you are doing?

Would you still do what you had planned to do for the next twenty-four hours? Pause and think about your schedule. Obligations. Engagements. Outings. Appointments. With Jesus taking over your heart, would anything change?

Keep working on this for a moment. Adjust the lens of your imagination until you have a clear picture of Jesus leading your life, then snap the shutter and frame the image. What you see is what God wants. He wants you to "think and act like Christ Jesus" (Phil. 2:5).

God's plan for you is nothing short of a new heart. If you were a car, God would want control of your engine. If you were a computer, God would claim the software and the hard drive. If you were an airplane, he'd take his seat in the cockpit. But you are a person, so God wants to change your heart.

"But you were taught to be made new in your hearts, to become a new person. That new person is made to be like God—made to be truly good and holy" (Eph. 4:23–24).

God wants you to be just like Jesus. He wants you to have a heart like his.

I'm going to risk something here. It's dangerous to sum up grand truths in one statement, but I'm going to try. If a sentence or two could capture God's desire for each of us, it might read like this:

> God loves you just the way you are, but he refuses to leave you that way. He wants you to be just like Jesus.

God loves you just the way you are. If you think his love for you would be stronger if your faith were, you are wrong. If you think his love would be deeper if your thoughts were, wrong again. Don't confuse God's love with the love of people. The love of people often increases with performance and decreases with mistakes. Not so with God's love. He loves you right where you are. To quote my wife's favorite author:

> God's love never ceases. Never. Though we spurn him. Ignore him. Reject him. Despise him. Disobey him. He will not change. Our evil cannot diminish his love. Our goodness cannot increase it. Our faith does not earn it anymore than our stupidity jeopardizes it. God doesn't love us less if we fail or more if we succeed. God's love never ceases.[1]

God loves you just the way you are, but he refuses to leave you that way.

When my daughter Jenna was a toddler, I used to take her to a park not far from our apartment. One day as she was playing in a sandbox, an ice-cream salesman approached us. I purchased her a treat, and when I turned to give it to her, I saw her mouth was full of sand. Where I intended to put a delicacy, she had put dirt.

Did I love her with dirt in her mouth? Absolutely. Was she any less my daughter with dirt in her mouth? Of course not. Was I going to allow her to keep the dirt in her mouth? No way. I loved her right where she was, but I refused to leave her there. I carried her over to the water fountain and washed out her mouth. Why? Because I love her.

God does the same for us. He holds us over the fountain. "Spit out the dirt, honey," our Father urges. "I've got something better for you." And so he cleanses us of filth: immorality, dishonesty, prejudice, bitterness, greed. We don't enjoy the cleansing; sometimes we even opt for the dirt over the ice cream. "I can eat dirt if I want to!" we pout and proclaim. Which is true—we can. But if we do, the loss is ours. God has a better offer. He wants us to be just like Jesus.

Isn't that good news? You aren't stuck with today's personality. You aren't condemned to "grumpydom." You are tweakable. Even if you've worried each day of your life, you needn't worry the rest of your life. So what if you were born a bigot? You don't have to die one.

Where did we get the idea we can't change? From whence come statements such as, "It's just my nature to worry," or, "I'll always be pessimistic. I'm just that way," or, "I have a bad temper. I can't help the way I react"? Who says? Would we make similar statements about our bodies? "It's just my nature to have a broken leg. I can't do anything about it." Of course not. If our bodies malfunction, we seek help. Shouldn't we do the same with our hearts? Shouldn't we seek aid for our sour attitudes? Can't we request treatment for our selfish tirades? Of course we can. Jesus can change our hearts. He wants us to have a heart like his.

Can you imagine a better offer?

THE HEART OF CHRIST

The heart of Jesus was pure. The Savior was adored by thousands, yet content to live a simple life. He was cared for by women (Luke 8:1–3), yet never accused of lustful thoughts; scorned by his own creation, but willing to forgive them before they even requested his mercy. Peter, who traveled with Jesus for three and a half years, described him as a "lamb, unblemished and spotless" (1 Pet. 1:19 NASB). After spending the same amount of time with Jesus, John concluded, "And in him is no sin" (1 John 3:5 NIV).

Jesus' heart was peaceful. The disciples fretted over the need to feed the thousands, but not Jesus. He thanked God for the problem. The disciples shouted for fear in the storm, but not Jesus. He slept through it. Peter drew his sword to fight the soldiers, but not Jesus. He lifted his hand to heal. His heart was at peace. When his disciples abandoned him, did he pout and go home? When Peter denied him, did Jesus lose his temper? When the soldiers spit in his face, did he breathe fire in theirs? Far from it. He was at peace. He forgave them. He refused to be guided by vengeance.

He also refused to be guided by anything other than his high call. His heart was purposeful. Most lives aim at nothing in particular and achieve it. Jesus aimed at one goal—to save humanity from its sin. He could summarize his life with one sentence: "The Son of man came to seek and to save the lost" (Luke 19:10 RSV). Jesus was so focused on his task that he knew when to say, "My time has not yet come" (John 2:4) and when to say, "It is finished" (John 19:30). But he was not so focused on his goal that he was unpleasant.

Quite the contrary. How pleasant were his thoughts! Children couldn't resist Jesus. He could find beauty in lilies, joy in worship, and possibilities in problems. He would spend days with multitudes of sick people and still feel sorry for them. He spent over three decades wading through the muck and mire of our sin yet still saw enough beauty in us to die for our mistakes.

But the crowning attribute of Christ was this: his heart was spiritual. His thoughts reflected his intimate relationship with the Father. "I am in the Father and the Father is in me," he stated (John 14:11). His first recorded sermon begins with the words, "The Spirit of the Lord is upon Me" (Luke 4:18 NASB). He was "led by the Spirit" (Matt. 4:1 NIV) and "full of the Holy Spirit" (Luke 4:1 NIV). He returned from the desert "in the power of the Spirit" (Luke 4:14 NIV).

Jesus took his instructions from God. It was his habit to go to worship (Luke 4:16). It was his practice to memorize scripture (Luke 4:4). Luke says Jesus "often slipped away to be alone so he could pray" (Luke 5:16). His times of prayer guided him. He once returned from prayer and announced it was time to move to another city (Mark 1:38). Another time of prayer resulted in the selection of the disciples (Luke 6:12–13). Jesus was led by an unseen hand. "The Son does whatever the Father does" (John 5:19). In the same chapter he stated, "I can do nothing alone. I judge only the way I am told" (John 5:30).

The heart of Jesus was spiritual.

THE HEART OF HUMANITY

Our hearts seem so far from his. He is pure; we are greedy. He is peaceful; we are hassled. He is purposeful; we are distracted. He is pleasant; we are cranky. He is spiritual; we are earthbound. The distance between our hearts and his seems so immense. How could we ever hope to have the heart of Jesus?

Ready for a surprise? You already do. You already have the heart of Christ. Why are you looking at me that way? Would I kid you? If you are in Christ, you already have the heart of Christ. One of the supreme yet unrealized promises of God is simply this: if you have given your life to Jesus, Jesus has given himself to you. He has made your heart his home. It would be hard to say it more succinctly than Paul does: "Christ lives in me" (Gal. 2:20 MSG).

At the risk of repeating myself, let me repeat myself. If you have given your life to Jesus, Jesus has given himself to you. He has moved in and unpacked his bags and is ready to change you "into his likeness from one degree of glory to another" (2 Cor. 3:18 RSV). Paul explains it with these words: "Strange as it seems, we Christians actually do have within us a portion of the very thoughts and mind of Christ" (1 Cor. 2:16 TLB).

Strange is the word! If I have the mind of Jesus, why do I still think so much like me? If I have the heart of Christ, why do I still have the hang-ups of Max? If Jesus dwells within me, why do I still hate traffic jams?

Part of the answer is illustrated in a story about a lady who had a small house on the seashore of Ireland at the turn of the century. She was quite wealthy but also quite frugal. The people were surprised, then, when she decided to be among the first to have electricity in her home.

Several weeks after the installation, a meter reader appeared at her door. He asked if her electricity was working well, and she assured him it was. "I'm wondering if you can explain something to me," he said. "Your meter shows scarcely any usage. Are you using your power?"

"Certainly," she answered. "Each evening when the sun sets, I turn on my lights just long enough to light my candles; then I turn them off."[2]

She's tapped into the power but doesn't use it. Her house is connected but not altered. Don't we make the same mistake? We, too—with our souls saved but our hearts unchanged—are connected but not altered. Trusting Christ for salvation but resisting transformation. We occasionally flip the switch, but most of the time we settle for shadows.

What would happen if we left the light on? What would

happen if we not only flipped the switch but lived in the light? What changes would occur if we set about the task of dwelling in the radiance of Christ?

No doubt about it: God has ambitious plans for us. The same one who saved your soul longs to remake your heart. His plan is nothing short of a total transformation: "He decided from the outset to shape the lives of those who love him along the same lines as the life of his Son" (Rom. 8:29 MSG).

"You have begun to live the new life, in which you are being made new and are becoming like the One who made you. This new life brings you the true knowledge of God" (Col. 3:10).

God is willing to change us into the likeness of the Savior. Shall we accept his offer? Here is my suggestion. Let's imagine what it means to be just like Jesus. Let's look long into the heart of Christ. Let's spend some chapters considering his compassion, reflecting upon his intimacy with the Father, admiring his focus, pondering his endurance. How did he forgive? When did he pray? What made him so pleasant? Why didn't he give up? Let's "fix our eyes on Jesus" (Heb. 12:2 NIV). Perhaps in seeing him, we will see what we can become.

Be gentle and ready to forgive;
never hold grudges. Remember, the Lord
forgave you, so you must forgive others.

COLOSSIANS 3:13 TLB

CHAPTER TWO

—❧❦❧—

LOVING THE PEOPLE
YOU ARE STUCK WITH

A Forgiving Heart

My first pet came in the form of a childhood Christmas Eve gift. Somewhere I have a snapshot of a brown-and-white Chinese pug, small enough to fit in my father's hand, cute enough to steal my eight-year-old heart. We named her Liz.

I carried her all day. Her floppy ears fascinated me, and her flat nose intrigued me. I even took her to bed. So what if she smelled like a dog? I thought the odor was cute. So what if she whined and whimpered? I thought the noise was cute. So what if she did her business on my pillow? Can't say I thought that was cute, but I didn't mind.

Mom and Dad had made it clear in our prenuptial agreement that I was to be Liz's caretaker, and I was happy to oblige. I cleaned her little eating dish and opened her can of puppy food. The minute she lapped up some water, I replenished it. I kept her hair combed and her tail wagging.

———

Within a few days, however, my feelings changed a bit. Liz was still my dog, and I was still her friend, but I grew weary with her barking, and she seemed hungry an awful lot. More than once my folks had to remind me, "Take care of her. She is your dog."

I didn't like hearing those words—*your dog*. I wouldn't have minded the phrase "your dog to play with" or "your dog when you want her" or even "your dog when she is behaving." But those weren't my parents' words. They said, "Liz is *your dog*." Period. In sickness and in health. For richer, for poorer. In dryness and in wetness.

That's when it occurred to me. *I am stuck with Liz*. The courtship was over, and the honeymoon had ended. We were mutually leashed. Liz went from an option to an obligation, from a pet to a chore, from someone to play with to someone to care for.

Perhaps you can relate. Chances are you know the claustrophobia that comes with commitment. Only instead of being reminded, "She is your dog," you're told, "He is your husband." Or, "She is your wife." Or, "He is your child, parent, employee or boss or roommate" or any other relationship that requires loyalty for survival.

Such permanence can lead to panic—at least it did in me. I had to answer some tough questions. Can I tolerate the same flat-nosed, hairy, hungry face every morning? (You wives know the feeling?) Am I going to be barked at until the day I die? (Any kids connecting here?) Will she ever learn to clean up her own mess? (Did I hear an "amen" from some parents?)

STUCKITITIS

Such are the questions we ask when we feel stuck with someone. There is a word for this condition. Upon consulting the one-word medical dictionary (which I wrote the day before I crafted this chapter), I discovered that this condition is a common malady known as *stuckititis*. (*Stuck* meaning "trapped." *Ititis* being the six letters you tag on to any word you want to sound impressive. Read it out loud: *stuckititis*.) *Max's Manual of Medical Terms* has this to say about the condition:

> Attacks of *stuckititis* are limited to people who breathe and typically occur somewhere between birth and death. *Stuckititis* manifests itself in irritability, short fuses, and a mountain range of molehills. The common symptom of *stuckititis* victims is the repetition of questions beginning with *who, what,* and *why. Who* is this person? *What* was I thinking? *Why* didn't I listen to my mother?[1]

This prestigious manual identifies three ways to cope with stuckititis: flee, fight, or forgive. Some opt to flee: to get out of the relationship and start again elsewhere, though they are often surprised when the condition surfaces on the other side of the fence as well. Others fight. Houses become combat zones, and offices become boxing rings, and tension becomes a way of life. A few, however, discover another treatment: forgiveness. My manual has no model for how forgiveness occurs, but the Bible does.

Jesus himself knew the feeling of being stuck with someone. For three years he ran with the same crew. By and large, he saw the same dozen or so faces around the table, around the campfire, around the clock. They rode in the same boats and walked the same roads and visited the same houses, and I wonder, how did Jesus stay so devoted to his men? Not only did he have to put up with their visible oddities, he had to endure their invisible foibles. Think about it. He could hear their unspoken thoughts. He knew their private doubts. Not only that, he knew their future doubts. What if you knew every mistake your loved ones had ever made and every mistake they would ever make? What if you knew every thought they would have about you, every irritation, every dislike, every betrayal?

Was it hard for Jesus to love Peter, knowing Peter would someday curse him? Was it tough to trust Thomas, knowing Thomas would one day question Jesus' resurrection? How did Jesus resist the urge to recruit a new batch of followers? John wanted to destroy one enemy. Peter sliced off the ear of another. Just days before Jesus' death, his disciples were arguing about which of them was the best! How was he able to love people who were hard to like?

Few situations stir panic like being trapped in a relationship. It's one thing to be stuck with a puppy but something else entirely to be stuck in a marriage. We may chuckle over goofy terms like *stuckititis,* but for many, this is no laughing matter. For that reason I think it wise that we begin our study of what it means to be just like Jesus by pondering his heart of forgiveness. How was Jesus able to love his disciples? The answer is found in the thirteenth chapter of John.

WITH TOWEL AND BASIN

Of all the times we see the bowing knees of Jesus, none is so precious as when he kneels before his disciples and washes their feet.

It was just before the Passover Feast. Jesus knew that the time had come for him to leave this world and go to the Father. Having loved his own who were in the world, he now showed them the full extent of his love.

> The evening meal was being served, and the devil had already prompted Judas Iscariot, son of Simon, to betray Jesus. Jesus knew that the Father had put all things under his power, and that he had come from God and was returning to God; so he got up from the meal, took off his outer clothing, . . . and began to wash his disciples' feet, drying them with the towel that was wrapped around him. (vv. 1–5 NIV)

It has been a long day. Jerusalem is packed with Passover guests, most of whom clamor for a glimpse of the Teacher. The spring sun is warm. The streets are dry. And the disciples are a long way from home. A splash of cool water would be refreshing.

The disciples enter, one by one, and take their places around the table. On the wall hangs a towel, and on the floor sits a pitcher and a basin. Any one of the disciples could volunteer for the job, but not one does.

After a few moments, Jesus stands and removes his outer garment. He wraps a servant's girdle around his waist, takes up the basin, and kneels before one of the disciples. He unlaces a sandal and gently lifts the foot and places it in the basin, covers it with water, and begins to bathe it. One by one, one grimy foot after another, Jesus works his way down the row.

In Jesus' day the washing of feet was a task reserved not just for servants but for the lowest of servants. Every circle has its pecking order, and the circle of household workers was no exception. The servant at the bottom of the totem pole was expected to be the one on his knees with the towel and basin.

In this case the one with the towel and basin is the king of the universe. Hands that shaped the stars now wash away filth. Fingers that formed mountains now massage toes. And the one before whom all nations will one day kneel now kneels before his disciples. Hours before his own death, Jesus' concern is singular. He wants his disciples to know how much he loves them. More than removing dirt, Jesus is removing doubt.

Jesus knows what will happen to his hands at the crucifixion. Within twenty-four hours they will be pierced and lifeless. Of all the times we'd expect him to ask for the disciples' attention, this would be one. But he doesn't.

You can be sure Jesus knows the future of these feet he is washing. These twenty-four feet will not spend the next day following their master, defending his cause. These feet will dash for cover at the flash of a Roman sword. Only one pair of feet won't abandon him in the garden. One disciple won't desert him at Gethsemane—Judas won't even make it that far! He will abandon Jesus that very night at the table.

I looked for a Bible translation that reads, "Jesus washed all the disciples' feet except the feet of Judas," but I couldn't find one. What a passionate moment when Jesus silently lifts the feet of his betrayer and washes them in the basin! Within hours the feet of Judas, cleansed by the kindness of the one he will betray, will stand in Caiaphas's court.

Behold the gift Jesus gives his followers! He knows what these men are about to do. He knows they are about to perform the vilest act of their lives. By morning they will bury their heads in shame and look down at their feet in disgust. And when they do, he wants them to remember how his knees knelt before them and he washed their feet. He wants them to realize those feet are still clean. "You don't understand now what I am doing, but you will understand later" (John 13:7).

Remarkable. He forgave their sin before they even committed it. He offered mercy before they even sought it.

FROM THE BASIN OF HIS GRACE

Oh, I could never do that, you object. *The hurt is so deep. The wounds are so numerous. Just seeing the person causes me to cringe.* Perhaps that is your problem. Perhaps you are seeing the wrong person or at least too much of the wrong person. Remember, the secret of being just like Jesus is "fixing our eyes" on him. Try shifting your glance away from the one who hurt you and setting your eyes on the one who has saved you.

Note the promise of John, "But if we live in the light, as God is in the light, we can share fellowship with each other. Then the blood of Jesus, God's Son, cleanses us from every sin" (1 John 1:7).

Aside from geography and chronology, our story is the same as the disciples'. We weren't in Jerusalem, and we weren't alive that night. But what Jesus did for them he has done for us. He has cleansed us. He has cleansed our hearts from sin.

Even more, he is still cleansing us! John tells us, "We are *being cleansed* from every sin by the blood of Jesus." In other words, we are *always being cleansed*. The cleansing is not a promise for the future but a reality in the present. Let a speck of dust fall on the soul of a saint, and it is washed away. Let a spot of filth land on the heart of God's child, and the filth is wiped away. Jesus still cleans his disciples' feet. Jesus still washes away stains. Jesus still purifies his people.

Our Savior kneels down and gazes upon the darkest acts of our lives. But rather than recoil in horror, he reaches out in kindness and says, "I can clean that if you want." And from the basin of his grace, he scoops a palm full of mercy and washes away our sin.

But that's not all he does. Because he lives in us, you and I can do the same. Because he has forgiven us, we can forgive others. Because he has a forgiving heart, we can have a forgiving heart. We can have a heart like his.

"If I, your Lord and Teacher, have washed your feet, you also should wash each other's feet. I did this as an example so that you should do as I have done for you" (John 13:14–15).

Jesus washes our feet for two reasons. The first is to give us mercy; the second is to give us a message, and that message is simply this: Jesus offers unconditional grace; we are to offer unconditional grace. The mercy of Christ preceded our mistakes; our mercy must precede the mistakes of others. Those in the circle of Christ had no doubt of his love; those in our circles should have no doubts about ours.

What does it mean to have a heart like his? It means to kneel as Jesus knelt, touching the grimy parts of the people we are stuck with and washing away their unkindnesses with kindness. Or as Paul wrote, "Be kind and loving to each other, and forgive each other just as God forgave you in Christ" (Eph. 4:32).

"But, Max," you are saying, "I've done nothing wrong. I'm not the one who cheated. I'm not the one who lied. I'm not the guilty party here." Perhaps you aren't. But neither was Jesus. Of all the men in that room, only one was worthy of having his feet washed. And he was the one who washed the feet. The one worthy of being served, served others. The genius of Jesus' example is that the burden of bridge-building falls on the strong one, not on the weak one. The one who is innocent is the one who makes the gesture.

And you know what happens? More often than not, if the one in the right volunteers to wash the feet of the one in the wrong, both parties get on their knees. Don't we all think we are right? Hence we wash each other's feet.

Please understand. *Relationships don't thrive because the guilty are punished but because the innocent are merciful.*

THE POWER OF FORGIVENESS

Recently I shared a meal with some friends. A husband and wife wanted to tell me about a storm they were weathering. Through a series of events, she learned of an act of infidelity that had occurred over a decade ago. He had made the mistake of thinking it'd be better not to tell her, so he didn't. But she found out. And as you can imagine, she was deeply hurt.

Through the advice of a counselor, the couple dropped everything and went away for several days. A decision had to be made. Would they flee, fight, or forgive? So they prayed. They talked. They walked. They reflected. In this case the wife was clearly in the right. She could have left. Women have done so for lesser reasons. Or she could have stayed and made his life a living hell. Other women have done that. But she chose a different response.

On the tenth night of their trip, my friend found a card on his pillow. On the card was a printed verse: "I'd rather do nothing with you than something without you." Beneath the verse she had written these words:

I forgive you. I love you. Let's move on.

The card might as well have been a basin. And the pen might as well have been a pitcher of water, for out of it poured pure mercy, and with it she washed her husband's feet.

Certain conflicts can be resolved only with a basin of water. Are any relationships in your world thirsty for mercy? Are there any sitting around your table who need to be assured of your grace? Jesus made sure his disciples had no reason to doubt his love. Why don't you do the same?

Since you have been chosen by God
who has given you this new kind of life,
and because of his deep love and concern
for you, you should practice tenderhearted
mercy and kindness to others.

COLOSSIANS 3:12 TLB

❧✦❧✦

CHAPTER THREE

THE TOUCH OF GOD

A Compassionate Heart

May I ask you to look at your hand for a moment? Look at the back, then the palm. Reacquaint yourself with your fingers. Run a thumb over your knuckles.

What if someone were to film a documentary on your hands? What if a producer were to tell your story based on the life of your hands? What would we see? As with all of us, the film would begin with an infant's fist, then a closeup of a tiny hand wrapped around mommy's finger. Then what? Holding on to a chair as you learned to walk? Handling a spoon as you learned to eat?

We aren't too long into the feature before we see your hand being affectionate, stroking daddy's face or petting a puppy. Nor is it too long before we see your hand acting aggressively: pushing big brother or yanking back a toy. All of us learned early that the hand is suited for more than survival—it's a tool

---

of emotional expression. The same hand can help or hurt, extend or clench, lift someone up or shove someone down.

Were you to show the documentary to your friends, you'd be proud of certain moments: your hand extending with a gift, placing a ring on another's finger, doctoring a wound, preparing a meal, or folding in prayer. And then there are other scenes. Shots of accusing fingers, abusive fists. Hands taking more often than giving, demanding instead of offering, wounding rather than loving. Oh, the power of our hands. Leave them unmanaged and they become weapons: clawing for power, strangling for survival, seducing for pleasure. But manage them and our hands become instruments of grace—not just tools in the hands of God, but *God's very hands.* Surrender them and these five-fingered appendages become the hands of heaven.

That's what Jesus did. Our Savior completely surrendered his hands to God. The documentary of his hands has no scenes of greedy grabbing or unfounded finger pointing. It does, however, have one scene after another of people longing for his compassionate touch: parents carrying their children, the poor bringing their fears, the sinful shouldering their sorrow. And each who came was touched. And each one touched was changed. But none was touched or changed more than the unnamed leper of Matthew 8.

> When Jesus came down from the hill, great crowds followed him. Then a man with a skin disease came to Jesus. The man bowed down before him and said, "Lord, you can heal me if you will."

Jesus reached out his hand and touched the man and said, "I will. Be healed!" And immediately the man was healed from his disease. Then Jesus said to him, "Don't tell anyone about this. But go and show yourself to the priest and offer the gift Moses commanded for people who are made well. This will show the people what I have done." (vv. 1–4)

Mark and Luke chose to tell this same story. But with apologies to all three writers, I must say none tell enough. Oh, we know the man's disease and his decision, but as to the rest? We are left with questions. The authors offer no name, no history, no description.

THE ULTIMATE OUTCAST

Sometimes my curiosity gets the best of me, and I wonder out loud. That's what I'm about to do here—wonder out loud about the man who felt Jesus' compassionate touch. He makes one appearance, has one request, and receives one touch. But that one touch changed his life forever. And I wonder if his story went something like this:

For five years no one touched me. No one. Not one person. Not my wife. Not my child. Not my friends. No one touched me. They saw me. They spoke to me. I sensed love in their voices. I saw concern in their eyes. But I didn't feel their touch. There was no touch. Not once. No one touched me.

What is common to you, I coveted. Handshakes. Warm embraces. A tap on the shoulder to get my attention. A kiss on the lips to steal a heart. Such moments were taken from my world. No one touched me. No one bumped into me. What I would have given to be bumped into, to be caught in a crowd, for my shoulder to brush against another's. But for five years it has not happened. How could it? I was not allowed on the streets. Even the rabbis kept their distance from me. I was not permitted in my synagogue. Not even welcome in my own house.

I was untouchable. I was a leper. And no one touched me. Until today.

I wonder about this man because in New Testament times leprosy was the most dreaded disease. The condition rendered the body a mass of ulcers and decay. Fingers would curl and gnarl. Blotches of skin would discolor and stink. Certain types of leprosy would numb nerve endings, leading to a loss of fingers, toes, even a whole foot or hand. Leprosy was death by inches.

The social consequences were as severe as the physical. Considered contagious, the leper was quarantined, banished to a leper colony.

In Scripture the leper is symbolic of the ultimate outcast: infected by a condition he did not seek, rejected by those he knew, avoided by people he did not know, condemned to a future he could not bear. And in the memory of each outcast must have been the day he was forced to face the truth: life would never be the same.

One year during harvest my grip on the scythe seemed weak. The tips of my fingers numbed. First one finger then another. Within a short time I could grip the tool but scarcely feel it. By the end of the season, I felt nothing at all. The hand grasping the handle might as well have belonged to someone else—the feeling was gone. I said nothing to my wife, but I know she suspected something. How could she not? I carried my hand against my body like a wounded bird.

One afternoon I plunged my hands into a basin of water intending to wash my face. The water reddened. My finger was bleeding, bleeding freely. I didn't even know I was wounded. How did I cut myself? On a knife? Did my hand slide across the sharp edge of metal? It must have, but I didn't feel anything.

"It's on your clothes, too," my wife said softly. She was behind me. Before looking at her, I looked down at the crimson spots on my robe. For the longest time I stood over the basin, staring at my hand. Somehow I knew my life was being forever altered.

"Shall I go with you to tell the priest?" she asked.

"No," I sighed, "I'll go alone."

I turned and looked into her moist eyes. Standing next to her was our three-year-old daughter. Squatting, I gazed into her face and stroked her cheek, saying nothing. What could I say? I stood and looked again at my wife. She touched my shoulder, and with my good hand, I touched hers. It would be our final touch.

Five years have passed, and no one has touched me since, until today.

The priest didn't touch me. He looked at my hand, now wrapped in a rag. He looked at my face, now shadowed in sorrow. I've never faulted him for what he said. He was only doing as he was instructed. He covered his mouth and extended his hand, palm forward. "You are unclean," he told me. With one pronouncement I lost my family, my farm, my future, my friends.

My wife met me at the city gates with a sack of clothing and bread and coins. She didn't speak. By now friends had gathered. What I saw *in their eyes was a precursor to what I've seen in every eye since: fearful pity. As I stepped out, they stepped back. Their horror of my disease was greater than their concern for my heart—so they, and everyone else I have seen since, stepped back.*

The banishing of a leper seems harsh, unnecessary. The Ancient East hasn't been the only culture to isolate their wounded, however. We may not build colonies or cover our mouths in their presence, but we certainly build walls and duck our eyes. And a person needn't have leprosy to feel quarantined.

One of my sadder memories involves my fourth-grade friend Jerry.[1] He and a half-dozen of us were an ever-present, inseparable fixture on the playground. One day I called his house to see if we could play. The phone was answered by a cursing, drunken voice telling me Jerry could not come over that day or any day. I told my friends what had happened. One of them explained that Jerry's father was an alcoholic. I don't know if I knew what the word meant, but I learned quickly. Jerry, the second baseman; Jerry, the kid with the red bike; Jerry, my friend on the corner was now "Jerry, the son of a drunk." Kids can be hard, and for some reason we were hard on Jerry. He was infected. Like the leper, he suffered from a condition he didn't create. Like the leper, he was put outside the village.

The divorced know this feeling. So do the handicapped. The unemployed have felt it, as have the less educated. Some shun unmarried moms. We keep our distance from the depressed and avoid the terminally ill. We have neighborhoods for immigrants, convalescent homes for the elderly, schools for the simple, centers for the addicted, and prisons for the criminals.

The rest simply try to get away from it all. Only God knows how many Jerrys are in voluntary exile—individuals living quiet, lonely lives infected by their fear of rejection and their memories of the last time they tried. They choose not to be touched at all rather than risk being hurt again.

Oh, how I repulsed those who saw me. Five years of leprosy had left my hands gnarled. Tips of my fingers were missing as were portions of an ear and my nose. At the sight of me, fathers grabbed their children. Mothers covered their faces. Children pointed and stared.

The rags on my body couldn't hide my sores. Nor could the wrap on my face hide the rage in my eyes. I didn't even try to hide it. How many nights did I shake my crippled fist at the silent sky? "What did I do to deserve this?" But never a reply.

Some think I sinned. Some think my parents sinned. I don't know. All I know is that I grew so tired of it all: sleeping in the colony, smelling the stench. I grew so tired of the damnable bell I was required to wear around my neck to warn people of my presence. As if I needed it. One glance and the announcements began, "Unclean! Unclean! Unclean!"

Several weeks ago I dared walk the road to my village. I had no intent of entering. Heaven knows I only wanted to look again upon my fields. Gaze again upon my home. And see, perchance, the face of my wife. I did not see her. But I saw some children playing in a pasture. I hid behind a tree and watched them scamper and run. Their faces were so joyful and their laughter so contagious that for a moment, for just a moment, I was no longer a leper. I was a farmer. I was a father. I was a man.

Infused with their happiness, I stepped out from behind the tree, straightened my back, breathed deeply . . . and they saw me. Before I could retreat, they saw me. And they screamed. And they scattered. One lingered, though, behind the others. One paused and looked in my direction. I don't know, and I can't say for sure, but I think, I really think, she was my daughter. And I don't know, I really can't say for sure. But I think she was looking for her father.

That look is what made me take the step I took today. Of course it was reckless. Of course it was risky. But what did I have to lose? He calls himself God's Son. Either he will hear my complaint and kill me or accept my demands and heal me. Those were my thoughts. I came to him as a defiant man. Moved not by faith but by a desperate anger. God had wrought this calamity on my body, and he would either fix it or end it.

But then I saw him, and when I saw him, I was changed. You must remember, I'm a farmer, not a poet, so I cannot find the words to describe what I saw. All I can say is that the Judean mornings are sometimes so fresh and the sunrises so glorious that to look at them is to forget the heat of the day before and the hurt of times past. When I looked at his face, I saw a Judean morning.

Before he spoke, I knew he cared. Somehow I knew he hated this disease as much as, no—more—than I hate it. My rage became trust, and my anger became hope.

From behind a rock, I watched him descend a hill. Throngs of people followed him. I waited until he was only paces from me, then I stepped out.

"Master!"

He stopped and looked in my direction as did dozens of others. A flood of fear swept across the crowd. Arms flew in front of faces. Chil-

dren ducked behind parents. "Unclean!" someone shouted. Again, I don't blame them. I was a huddled mass of death. But I scarcely heard them. I scarcely saw them. Their panic I'd seen a thousand times. His compassion, however, I'd never beheld. Everyone stepped back except him. He stepped toward me. Toward me.

Five years ago my wife had stepped toward me. She was the last to do so. Now he did. I did not move. I just spoke. "Lord, you can heal me if you will." Had he healed me with a word, I would have been thrilled. Had he cured me with a prayer, I would have rejoiced. But he wasn't satisfied with speaking to me. He drew near me. He touched me. Five years ago my wife had touched me. No one had touched me since. Until today.

"I will." His words were as tender as his touch. "Be healed!"

Energy flooded my body like water through a furrowed field. In an instant, in a moment, I felt warmth where there had been numbness. I felt strength where there had been atrophy. My back straightened, and my head lifted. Where I had been eye level with his belt, I now stood eye level with his face. His smiling face.

He cupped his hands on my cheeks and drew me so near I could feel the warmth of his breath and see the wetness in his eyes. "Don't tell anyone about this. But go and show yourself to the priest and offer the gift Moses commanded for people who are made well. This will show the people what I have done."

And so that is where I am going. I will show myself to my priest and embrace him. I will show myself to my wife, and I will embrace her. I will pick up my daughter, and I will embrace her. And I will never forget the one who dared to touch me. He could have healed me with a word. But he wanted to do more than heal me. He wanted to honor me, *to validate me, to christen me. Imagine that . . . unworthy of the touch of a man, yet worthy of the touch of God.*

THE POWER OF THE GODLY TOUCH

The touch did not heal the disease, you know. Matthew is careful to mention that it was the pronouncement and not the touch of Christ that cured the condition. "Jesus reached out his hand and touched the man and said, 'I will. Be healed!' And immediately the man was healed from his disease" (Matt. 8:3).

The infection was banished by a word from Jesus.

The loneliness, however, was treated by a touch from Jesus.

Oh, the power of a godly touch. Haven't you known it? The doctor who treated you, or the teacher who dried your tears? Was there a hand holding yours at a funeral? Another on your shoulder during a trial? A handshake of welcome at a new job? A pastoral prayer for healing? Haven't we known the power of a godly touch?

Can't we offer the same?

Many of you already do. Some of you have the master touch of the Physician himself. You use your hands to pray over the sick and minister to the weak. If you aren't touching them personally, your hands are writing letters, dialing phones, baking pies. You have learned the power of a touch.

But others of us tend to forget. Our hearts are good; it's just that our memories are bad. We forget how significant one touch can be. We fear saying the wrong thing or using the wrong tone or acting the wrong way. So rather than do it incorrectly, we do nothing at all.

Aren't we glad Jesus didn't make the same mistake? If your fear of doing the wrong thing prevents you from doing anything, keep in mind the perspective of the lepers of the world. They aren't picky. They aren't finicky. They're just lonely. They are yearning for a godly touch.

Jesus touched the untouchables of the world. Will you do the same?

Do not merely listen to the word,
and so deceive yourselves. Do what it says.
Anyone who listens to the word but does
not do what it says is like a man who looks
at his face in a mirror and, after looking
at himself, goes away and immediately
forgets what he looks like.

JAMES 1:22—24 NIV

CHAPTER FOUR

HEARING GOD'S MUSIC

A Listening Heart

"Let he who has ears to hear, use them."

More than once Jesus said these words. Eight times in the Gospels and eight times in the Book of Revelation[1] we are reminded that it's not enough just to have ears—it's necessary to use them.

In one of his parables[2] Jesus compared our ears to soil. He told about a farmer who scattered seed (symbolic of the Word) in four different types of ground (symbolic of our ears). Some of our ears are like a hard road—unreceptive to the seed. Others have ears like rocky soil—we hear the Word but don't allow it to take root. Still others have ears akin to a weed patch—too overgrown, too thorny, with too much competition for the seed to have a chance. And then there are some who have ears that hear: well tilled, discriminate, and ready to hear God's voice.

Please note that in all four cases the seed is the same seed. The sower is the same sower. What's different is not the message or the messenger—it's the listener. And if the ratio in the story is significant, three-fourths of the world isn't listening to God's voice. Whether the cause be hard hearts, shallow lives, or anxious minds, 75 percent of us are missing the message.

It's not that we don't have ears; it's that we don't use them.

Scripture has always placed a premium on hearing God's voice. Indeed, the great command from God through Moses began with the words, "Hear, O Israel: the LORD our God is one LORD" (Deut. 6:4 KJV). Nehemiah and his men were commended because they were "attentive unto the book of the Law" (Neh. 8:3 KJV). "Happy are those who listen to me" is the promise of Proverbs 8:34. Jesus urges us to learn to listen like sheep. "The sheep recognize his voice. . . . they follow because they are familiar with [the shepherd's] voice. They won't follow a stranger's voice but will scatter because they aren't used to the sound of it" (John 10:3–5 MSG). Each of the seven churches in Revelation is addressed in the same manner: "He who has an ear, let him hear what the Spirit says to the churches."[3]

Our ears, unlike our eyes, do not have lids. They are to remain open, but how easily they close.

Denalyn and I were shopping for luggage sometime back. We found what we wanted in one store and told the salesclerk we were going to another store to compare prices. He asked me if I wanted to take his business card. I told him, "No, your name is easy to remember, Bob."

To which he replied, "My name is Joe."

I had heard the man, but I hadn't listened.

Pilate didn't listen either. He had the classic case of ears that didn't hear. Not only did his wife warn him, "Don't do anything to that man, because he is innocent" (Matt. 27:19), but the very Word of Life stood before Pilate in his chamber and proclaimed, "Everyone who belongs to the truth listens to me" (John 18:37). But Pilate had selective hearing. He allowed the voices of the people to dominate the voices of conscience and the carpenter. "Their voices prevailed" (Luke 23:23 RSV).

In the end Pilate inclined his ear to the crowd and away from the Christ and ignored the message of the Messiah. "Faith comes from hearing" (Rom. 10:17), and since Pilate didn't hear, he never found faith.

"Let he who has ears to hear, use them." How long has it been since you had your hearing checked? When God throws seed your way, what is the result? May I raise a question or two to test how well you hear God's voice?

HOW LONG HAS IT BEEN
SINCE YOU LET GOD HAVE YOU?

I mean really *have* you? How long since you gave him a portion of undiluted, uninterrupted time listening for his voice? Apparently Jesus did. He made a deliberate effort to spend time with God.

Spend much time reading about the listening life of Jesus and a distinct pattern emerges. He spent regular time with God, praying and listening. Mark says, "Very early in the morning, while it was still dark, Jesus got up, left the house and went off to a solitary place, where he prayed" (Mark 1:35 NIV). Luke tells us, "Jesus often withdrew to lonely places and prayed" (Luke 5:16 NIV).

Let me ask the obvious. If Jesus, the Son of God, the sinless Savior of humankind, thought it worthwhile to clear his calendar to pray, wouldn't we be wise to do the same?

Not only did he spend regular time with God in prayer, he spent regular time in God's Word. Of course we don't find Jesus pulling a leather-bound New Testament from his satchel and reading it. We do, however, see the stunning example of Jesus, in the throes of the wilderness temptation, using the Word of God to deal with Satan. Three times he is tempted, and each time he repels the attack with the phrase: "It is written in the Scriptures" (Luke 4:4,8,12), and then he quotes a verse. Jesus is so familiar with Scripture that he not only knows the verse, he knows how to use it.

And then there's the occasion when Jesus was asked to read in the synagogue. He is handed the book of Isaiah the prophet. He finds the passage, reads it, and declares, "While you heard these words just now, they were coming true!" (Luke 4:21). We are given the picture of a person who knows his way around in Scripture and can recognize its fulfillment. If Jesus thought it wise to grow familiar with the Bible, shouldn't we do the same?

If we are to be just like Jesus—if we are to have ears that hear God's voice—then we have just found two habits worth imitating: the habits of prayer and Bible reading. Consider these verses:

Base your happiness on your hope in Christ. When trials come endure them patiently; steadfastly maintain *the habit of prayer*. (Rom. 12:12 PHILLIPS, italics mine)

The man who looks into the perfect law, the law of liberty, and makes a habit of so doing, is not the man who hears and forgets. He puts that law into practice and he wins true happiness. (James 1:25 PHILLIPS)

If we are to be just like Jesus, we must have a regular time of talking to God and listening to his Word.

SURROGATE SPIRITUALITY

Wait a minute. Don't you do that. I know exactly what some of you are doing. You are tuning me out. *Lucado is talking about daily devotionals, eh? This is a good time for me to take a mental walk over to the fridge and see what we have to eat.*

I understand your reluctance. Some of us have tried to have a daily quiet time and have not been successful. Others of us have a hard time concentrating. And all of us are busy. So rather than spend time with God, listening for his voice, we'll let others spend time with him and then benefit from their experience. Let them tell us what God is saying. After all, isn't that why we pay preachers? Isn't that why we read Christian books? *These folks are good at daily devotions. I'll just learn from them.*

If that is your approach, if your spiritual experiences are secondhand and not firsthand, I'd like to challenge you with this thought: Do you do that with other parts of your life? I don't think so.

You don't do that with vacations. You don't say, "Vacations are such a hassle, packing bags and traveling. I'm going to send someone on vacation for me. When he returns, I'll hear all about it and be spared all the inconvenience." Would you do that? No! You want the experience firsthand. You want the sights firsthand, and you want to rest firsthand. Certain things no one can do for you.

You don't do that with romance. You don't say, "I'm in love with that wonderful person, but romance is such a hassle. I'm going to hire a surrogate lover to enjoy the romance in my place. I'll hear all about it and be spared the inconvenience." Who would do that? Perish the thought. You want the romance firsthand. You don't want to miss a word or a date, and you certainly don't want to miss the kiss, right? Certain things no one can do for you.

You don't let someone eat on your behalf, do you? You don't say, "Chewing is such a bother. My jaws grow so tired, and the variety of tastes is so overwhelming. I'm going to hire someone to chew my food, and I'll just swallow whatever he gives me." Would you do that? Yuck! Of course not! Certain things no one can do for you.

And one of those is spending time with God.

Listening to God is a firsthand experience. When he asks for your attention, God doesn't want you to send a substitute; he wants you. He invites *you* to vacation in his splendor. He invites *you* to feel the touch of his hand. He invites *you* to feast at his table. He wants to spend time with *you*. And with a little training, your time with God can be the highlight of your day.

A friend of mine married an opera soprano. She loves concerts. Her college years were spent in the music department, and her earliest memories are of keyboards and choir risers. He, on the other hand, leans more toward Monday Night Football and country music. He also loves his wife, so on occasion he attends an opera. The two sit side by side in the same auditorium, listening to the same music, with two completely different responses. He sleeps and she weeps.

I believe the difference is more than taste. It's training. She has spent hours learning to appreciate the art of music. He has spent none. Her ears are Geiger-counter sensitive. He can't differentiate between *staccato* and *legato*. But he is trying. Last time we talked about the concerts, he told me he is managing to stay awake. He may never have the same ear as his wife, but with time he is learning to listen and appreciate the music.

LEARNING TO LISTEN

I believe we can, too. Equipped with the right tools, we can learn to listen to God. What are those tools? Here are the ones I have found helpful.

A regular time and place. Select a slot on your schedule and a corner of your world, and claim it for God. For some it may be best to do this in the morning. "In the morning my prayer comes before you" (Ps. 88:13 NIV). Others prefer the evening and agree with David's prayer, "Let my . . . praise [be] like the evening sacrifice" (Ps. 141:2). Others prefer many encounters during the day. Apparently the author of Psalm 55 did. He wrote, "Evening, morning and noon I cry out" (v. 17 NIV).

Some sit under a tree, others in the kitchen. Maybe your commute to work or your lunch break would be appropriate. Find a time and place that seems right for you.

How much time should you take? As much as you need. Value quality over length. Your time with God should last long enough for you to say what you want and for God to say what he wants. Which leads us to a second tool you need—*an open Bible*.

God speaks to us through his Word. The first step in reading the Bible is to ask God to help you understand it. "But the Helper will teach you everything and will cause you to remember all that I told you. This Helper is the Holy Spirit whom the Father will send in my name" (John 14:26).

Before reading the Bible, pray. Don't go to Scripture looking for your own idea; go searching for God's. Read the Bible prayerfully. Also, read the Bible carefully. Jesus told us, "Search, and you will find" (Matt. 7:7). God commends those who "chew on Scripture day and night" (Ps. 1:2 MSG). The Bible is not a newspaper to be skimmed but rather a mine to be quarried. "Search for it like silver, and hunt for it like hidden treasure. Then you will understand respect for the LORD, and you will find that you know God" (Prov. 2:4–5).

Here is a practical point. Study the Bible a little at a time. God seems to send messages as he did his manna: one day's portion at a time. He provides "a command here, a command there. A rule here, a rule there. A little lesson here, a little lesson there" (Isa. 28:10). Choose depth over quantity. Read until a verse "hits" you, then stop and meditate on it. Copy the verse onto a sheet of paper, or write it in your journal, and reflect on it several times.

On the morning I wrote this, for example, my quiet time found me in Matthew 18. I was only four verses into the chapter when I read, *The greatest person in the kingdom of heaven is the one who makes himself humble like this child.* I needed to go no further. I copied the words in my journal and have pondered them on and off during the day. Several times I asked God, "How can I be more childlike?" By the end of the day, I was reminded of my tendency to hurry and my proclivity to worry.

Will I learn what God intends? If I listen, I will.

Don't be discouraged if your reading reaps a small harvest. Some days a lesser portion is all we need. A little girl returned from her first day at school. Her mom asked, "Did you learn anything?" "I guess not," the girl responded. "I have to go back tomorrow and the next day and the next day . . ."

Such is the case with learning. And such is the case with Bible study. Understanding comes a little at a time over a lifetime.

There is a third tool for having a productive time with God. Not only do we need a regular time and an open Bible, we also need *a listening heart.* Don't forget the admonition from James: "The man who looks into the perfect law, the law of liberty, and makes a habit of so doing, is not the man who hears and forgets. He puts that law into practice and he wins true happiness" (James 1:25 PHILLIPS).

We know we are listening to God when what we read in the Bible is what others see in our lives. Perhaps you've heard the story of the not-so-bright fellow who saw an advertisement for a cruise. The sign in the travel agency window read "Cruise—$100 Cash."

I've got a hundred dollars, he thought. *And I'd like to go on a cruise.* So he entered the door and announced his desires. The fellow at the desk asked for the money, and the not-too-bright guy started counting it out. When he got to one hundred, he was whacked over the head and knocked out cold. He woke up in a barrel floating down a river. Another sucker in another barrel floated past and asked him, "Say, do they serve lunch on this cruise?"

The not-too-bright fellow answered, "They didn't last year."

It's one thing not to know. It's another to know and not learn. Paul urged his readers to put into practice what they had learned from him. "What you have learned and received and heard and seen in me, do" (Phil. 4:9 RSV).

If you want to be just like Jesus, let God have you. Spend time listening for him until you receive your lesson for the day—then apply it.

I have another question to check your hearing. Read it, and see how well you do.

HOW LONG SINCE YOU LET GOD LOVE YOU?

My daughters are too old for this now, but when they were young—crib-size and diaper-laden—I would come home, shout their names, and watch them run to me with extended arms and squealing voices. For the next few moments we would speak the language of love. We'd roll on the floor, gobble bellies, and tickle tummies and laugh and play.

We delighted in each other's presence. They made no requests of me, with the exception of "Let's play, Daddy." And I made no demands of them, except, "Don't hit Daddy with the hammer."

My kids let me love them.

But suppose my daughters had approached me as we often approach God. "Hey, Dad, glad you're home. Here is what I want. More toys. More candy. And can we go to Disneyland this summer?"

"Whoa," I would have wanted to say. "I'm not a waiter, and this isn't a restaurant. I'm your father, and this is our house. Why don't you just climb up on Daddy's lap and let me tell you how much I love you?"

Ever thought God might want to do the same with you? *Oh, he wouldn't say that to me.* He wouldn't? Then to whom was he speaking when he said, "I have loved you with an everlasting love" (Jer. 31:3 NIV)? Was he playing games when he said, "Nothing . . . will ever be able to separate us from the love of God that is in Christ" (Rom. 8:39)? Buried in the seldom-quarried mines of the minor prophets is this jewel:

> The LORD your God is with you; the mighty One will save you. He will rejoice over you. You will rest in his love; he will sing and be joyful about you. (Zeph. 3:17)

Don't move too quickly through that verse. Read it again and prepare yourself for a surprise.

> The LORD your God is with you; the mighty One will save
> you. He will rejoice over you. You will rest in his love; he
> will sing and be joyful about you. (Zeph. 3:17)

Note who is active and who is passive. Who is singing, and who is resting? Who is rejoicing over his loved one, and who is being rejoiced over?

We tend to think we are the singers and God is the "singee." Most certainly that is often the case. But apparently there are times when God wishes we would just be still and (what a stunning thought!) let him sing over us.

I can see you squirming. You say you aren't worthy of such affection? Neither was Judas, but Jesus washed his feet. Neither was Peter, but Jesus fixed him breakfast. Neither were the Emmaus-bound disciples, but Jesus took time to sit at their table.

Besides, who are we to determine if we are worthy? Our job is simply to be still long enough to let him have us and let him love us.

DO YOU HEAR THE MUSIC?

I'm going to conclude by telling you a story you've heard before, though you've not heard it as I am going to tell it. But you have heard it. Surely you have, for you are in it. You are one of the characters. It is the story of the dancers who had no music.

Can you imagine how hard that would be? Dancing with no music? Day after day they came to the great hall just off the corner of Main and Broadway. They brought their wives. They brought their husbands. They brought their children and their hopes. They came to dance.

The hall was prepared for a dance. Streamers strung, punch bowls filled. Chairs were placed against the walls. People arrived and sat, knowing they had come to a dance but not knowing how to dance because they had no music. They had balloons; they had cake. They even had a stage on which the musicians could play, but they had no musicians.

One time a lanky fellow claimed to be a musician. He sure looked the part, what with his belly-length beard and fancy violin. All stood the day he stood before them and pulled the violin out of the case and placed it beneath his chin. *Now we will dance,* they thought, but they were wrong. For though he had a violin, his violin had no strings. The pushing and pulling of his bow sounded like the creaking of an unoiled door. Who can dance to a sound like that? So the dancers took their seats again.

Some tried to dance without the music. One wife convinced her husband to give it a try, so out on the floor they stepped, she dancing her way and he dancing his. Both efforts were commendable—but far from compatible. He danced some form of partnerless tango, while she was spinning like a ballerina. A few tried to follow their cue, but since there was no cue, they didn't know how to follow. The result was a dozen or so dancers with no music, going this way and that, bumping into each other and causing more than one observer to seek safety behind a chair.

Over time, however, those dancers grew weary, and everyone resumed the task of sitting and staring and wondering if anything was ever going to happen. And then one day it did.

Not everyone saw him enter. Only a few. Nothing about his appearance would compel your attention. His looks were common, but his music was not. He began to sing a song, soft and sweet, kind and compelling. His song took the chill out of the air and brought a summer-sunset glow to the heart.

And as he sang, people stood—a few at first, then many—and they began to dance. Together. Flowing to a music they had never heard before, they danced.

Some, however, remained seated. What kind of musician is this who never mounts the stage? Who brings no band? Who has no costume? Why, musicians don't just walk in off the street. They have an entourage, a reputation, a persona to project and protect. Why, this fellow scarcely mentioned his name!

"How can we know what you sing is actually music?" they challenged.

His reply was to the point: "Let the man who has ears to hear use them."

But the nondancers refused to hear. So they refused to dance. Many still refuse. The musician comes and sings. Some dance. Some don't. Some find music for life; others live in silence. To those who miss the music, the musician gives the same appeal: "Let the man who has ears to hear use them."

A regular time and place.
An open Bible.
An open heart.

Let God have you, and let God love you—and don't be surprised if your heart begins to hear music you've never heard
and your feet learn to dance as never before.

*I will be in them and you
will be in me so that they will be
completely one. Then the world will know
that you sent me and that you loved
them just as much as you loved me.*

JOHN 17:23

CHAPTER FIVE

BEING LED BY
AN UNSEEN HAND

A God-Intoxicated Heart

It's a wonderful day indeed when we stop working for God and begin working with God. (Go ahead, read the sentence again.)

For years I viewed God as a compassionate CEO and my role as a loyal sales representative. He had his office, and I had my territory. I could contact him as much as I wanted. He was always a phone or fax away. He encouraged me, rallied behind me, and supported me, but he didn't go with me. At least I didn't think he did. Then I read 2 Corinthians 6:1: We are "God's fellow workers" (NIV).

Fellow workers? Colaborers? God and I work together? Imagine the paradigm shift this truth creates. Rather than report to God, we work *with* God. Rather than check in with him and then leave, we check in with him and then follow. We are always in the presence of God. We never leave church. There is never a nonsacred moment! His presence never diminishes. Our awareness of his presence may falter, but the reality of his presence never changes.

This leads me to a great question. If God is perpetually present, is it possible to enjoy unceasing communion with him? In the last chapter we discussed the importance of setting aside daily time to spend with God. Let's take the thought a step further. A giant step further. What if our daily communion never ceased? Would it be possible to live—*minute by minute*—in the presence of God? Is such intimacy even possible? One man who wrestled with these questions wrote:

> Can we have that contact with God all the time? All the time awake, fall asleep in His arms, and awaken in His presence? Can we attain that? Can we do His will all the time? Can we think His thoughts all the time? . . . Can I bring the Lord back in my mind-flow every few seconds so that God shall always be in my mind? I choose to make the rest of my life an experiment in answering this question.[1]

The words are found in the journal of Frank Laubach. Born in the United States in 1884, he was a missionary to the illiterate, teaching them to read so they could know the beauty of the Scriptures. What fascinates me about this man, however, is not his teaching. I'm fascinated by his listening. Dissatisfied with his spiritual life, at the age of forty-five Laubach resolved to live in "continuous inner conversation with God and in perfect responsiveness to His will."[2]

He chronicled this experiment, begun on January 30, 1930, in his journal. Laubach's words have inspired me so much, I've included some key passages here. As you read them, keep in mind that they were not penned by a monk in a monastery but by a busy, dedicated instructor. By the time he died in 1970, Laubach and his techniques of education were known on almost every continent. He was widely respected and widely traveled. The desire of his heart was not recognition, however, but unbroken communion with the Father.

JANUARY 26, 1930: I am feeling God in each movement, by an act of will—willing that He shall direct these fingers that now strike this typewriter—willing that He shall pour through my steps as I walk.

MARCH 1, 1930: This sense of being led by an unseen hand which takes mine while another hand reaches ahead and prepares the way, grows upon me daily. . . . sometimes it requires a long time early in the morning. I determine not to get out of bed until that mind set upon the Lord is settled.

APRIL 18, 1930: I have tasted a thrill in fellowship with God which has made anything discordant with God disgusting. This afternoon the possession of God has caught me up with such sheer joy that I thought I never had known anything like it. God was so close and so amazingly lovely that I felt like melting all over with a strange blissful contentment. Having had this experience, which comes to me now several times a week, the thrill of filth repels me, for I know its power to drag me from God. And after an hour of close friendship with God my soul feels clean, as new fallen snow.

MAY 14, 1930: Oh, this thing of keeping in constant touch with God, of making Him the object of my thought and the companion of my conversations, is the most amazing thing I ever ran across. It is working. I cannot do it even half of a day—not yet, but I believe I shall be doing it some day for the entire day. It is a matter of acquiring a new habit of thought.

MAY 24, 1930: This concentration upon God is strenuous, but everything else has ceased to be so. I think more clearly, I forget less frequently. Things which I did with a strain before, I now do easily and with no effort whatever. I worry about nothing, and lose no sleep. I walk on air a good part of the time. Even the mirror reveals a new light in my eyes and face. I no longer feel in a hurry about anything. Everything goes right. Each minute I meet calmly as though it were not important. Nothing can go wrong excepting one thing. That is that God may slip from my mind.

JUNE 1, 1930: Ah, God, what a new nearness this brings for Thee and me, to realize that Thou alone canst understand me, for Thou alone knowest all! Thou art no longer a stranger, God! Thou art the only being in the universe who is not partly a stranger! Thou art all the way inside with me—here. . . . I mean to struggle tonight and tomorrow as never before, not once to dismiss thee. For when I lose Thee for an hour I lose. The thing Thou wouldst do can only be done when Thou hast full sway all the time.

Last Monday was the most completely successful day of my life to date, so far as giving my day in complete and continuous surrender to God is concerned. . . . I remember how as I looked at people with a love God gave, they looked back and acted as though they wanted to go with me. I felt then that for a day I saw a little of that marvelous pull that Jesus had as He walked along the road day after day "God-intoxicated" and radiant with the endless communion of His soul with God.[3]

What do you think of Frank Laubach's adventure? How would you answer his questions? *Can we have that contact with God all the time? All the time awake, fall asleep in His arms, and awaken in His presence? Can we attain that?*

Is such a goal realistic? Within reach? Or do you think the idea of constant fellowship with God is somewhat fanatical, even extreme? Whatever your opinion of Laubach's adventure, you have to agree with his observation that Jesus enjoyed unbroken communion with God. And if we are to be just like Jesus, you and I will strive to do the same.

GOD'S TRANSLATOR

Jesus' relationship with God went far deeper than a daily appointment. Our Savior was always aware of his father's presence. Listen to his words:

> The Son can do nothing on his own, but only what he sees the Father doing; for whatever the Father does, the Son does likewise. (John 5:19 NRSV)

> I can do nothing on my own. As I hear, I judge. (John 5:30 NRSV)

> I am in the Father and the Father is in me. (John 14:11 NRSV)

Clearly, Jesus didn't act unless he saw his father act. He didn't judge until he heard his father judge. No act or deed occurred without his father's guidance. His words have the ring of a translator.

There were a few occasions in Brazil when I served as a translator for an English speaker. He stood before the audience, complete with the message. I stood at his side, equipped with the language. My job was to convey his story to the listeners. I did my best to allow his words to come through me. I was not at liberty to embellish or subtract. When the speaker gestured, I gestured. As his volume increased, so did mine. When he got quiet, I did, too.

When he walked this earth, Jesus was "translating" God all the time. When God got louder, Jesus got louder. When God gestured, Jesus gestured. He was so in sync with the Father that he could declare, "I am in the Father and the Father is in me" (John 14:11 NRSV). It was as if he heard a voice others were missing.

I witnessed something similar to this on an airplane once. I kept hearing outbursts of laughter. The flight was turbulent and bumpy, hardly a reason for humor. But some fellow behind me was cracking up. No one else, just him. Finally I turned to see what was so funny. He was wearing headphones and apparently listening to a comedian. Because he could hear what I couldn't, he acted differently than I did.

The same was true with Jesus. Because he could hear what others couldn't, he acted differently than they did. Remember when everyone was troubled about the man born blind? Jesus wasn't. Somehow he knew that the blindness would reveal God's power (John 9:3). Remember when everyone was distraught about Lazarus's illness? Jesus wasn't. Rather than hurry to his friend's bedside, he said, "This sickness will not end in death. It is for the glory of God, to bring glory to the son of God" (John 11:4). It was as if Jesus could hear what no one else could. How could a relationship be more intimate? Jesus had unbroken communion with his father.

Do you suppose the Father desires the same for us? Absolutely. Paul says we have been "predestined to be conformed to the image of his Son" (Rom. 8:29 NRSV). Let me remind you: God loves you just the way you are, but he refuses to leave you that way. He wants you to be just like Jesus. God desires the same abiding intimacy with you that he had with his son.

PICTURES OF INTIMACY

God draws several pictures to describe the relationship he envisions. One is of a vine and a branch.

> I am the vine, and you are the branches. If any remain in me and I remain in them, they produce much fruit. But without me they can do nothing. . . . If you remain in me and follow my teachings, you can ask anything you want, and it will be given to you. (John 15:5,7)

God wants to be as close to us as a branch is to a vine. One is an extension of the other. It's impossible to tell where one starts and the other ends. The branch isn't connected only at the moment of bearing fruit. The gardener doesn't keep the branches in a box and then, on the day he wants grapes, glue them to the vine. No, the branch constantly draws nutrition from the vine. Separation means certain death.

God also uses the temple to depict the intimacy he desires. "Don't you know," Paul writes, "that your body is the temple of the Holy Spirit, who lives in you and was given to you by God?" (1 Cor. 6:19 TEV). Think with me about the temple for a moment. Was God a visitor or a resident in Solomon's temple? Would you describe his presence as occasional or permanent? You know the answer. God didn't come and go, appear and disappear. He was a permanent presence, always available.

What incredibly good news for us! We are NEVER away from God! He is NEVER away from us—not even for a moment! God doesn't come to us on Sunday mornings and then exit on Sunday afternoons. He remains within us, continually present in our lives.

The biblical analogy of marriage is the third picture of this encouraging truth. Aren't we the bride of Christ (Rev. 21:2)? Aren't we united with him (Rom. 6:5 RSV)? Haven't we made vows to him, and hasn't he made vows to us?

What does our marriage to Jesus imply about his desire to commune with us? For one thing, the communication never stops. In a happy home the husband doesn't talk to the wife only when he wants something from her. He doesn't pop in just when he wants a good meal or a clean shirt or a little romance. If he does, the home is not a home—it's a brothel that serves food and cleans clothes.

Healthy marriages have a sense of "remaining." The husband remains in the wife, and she remains in him. There is a tenderness, an honesty, an ongoing communication. The same is true in our relationship with God. Sometimes we go to him with our joys, and sometimes we go with our hurts, but we always go. And as we go, the more we go, the more we become like him. Paul says we are being changed from "glory to glory" (2 Cor. 3:18 KJV).

People who live long lives together eventually begin to sound alike, to talk alike, even to think alike. As we walk with God, we take on his thoughts, his principles, his attitudes. We take on his heart.

And just as in marriage, communion with God is no burden. Indeed, it is a delight. "How lovely is your dwelling place, O LORD Almighty! My soul yearns, even faints, for the courts of the LORD; my heart and my flesh cry out for the living God" (Ps. 84:1–2 NIV). The level of communication is so sweet nothing compares with it. Laubach wrote:

> It is my business to look into the very face of God until I ache with bliss. . . . Now I like the Lord's presence so much that when for a half hour or so He slips out of mind—as He does many times a day—I feel as though I had deserted Him, and as though I had lost something very precious in my life. (March 3, 1931; May 14, 1930)[4]

Can we consider one last analogy from the Bible? How about the sheep with the shepherd? Many times Scripture calls us the flock of God. "We are his people, the sheep he tends" (Ps. 100:3). We needn't know much about sheep to know that the shepherd never leaves the flock. If we see a flock coming down the path, we know a shepherd is nearby. If we see a Christian ahead, we can know the same. The Good Shepherd never leaves his sheep. "Even though I walk through a very dark valley, I will not be afraid, because you are with me" (Ps. 23:4).

God is as near to you as the vine is to the branch, as present within you as God was in the temple, as intimate with you as a husband with a wife, and as devoted to you as a shepherd to his sheep.

God desires to be as close to you as he was to Christ—
so close that he can literally speak through you and
all you need do is translate;

so close that tuning in to him is like putting on headphones;
  so close that when others sense the storm and worry,
    you hear his voice and smile.

Here is how King David described this most intimate of all relationships:

I'm an open book to you;
  even from a distance, you know what I'm thinking.
You know when I leave and when I get back;
  I'm never out of your sight.
You know everything I'm going to say
  before I start the first sentence.
I look behind me and you're there,
  then up ahead and you're there, too—
  your reassuring presence, coming and going.
This is too much, too wonderful—
  I can't take it all in! (Ps. 139:1–6 MSG)

David wasn't the only Bible writer to testify to the possibility of a constant sense of God's presence. Consider these staccato statements from the pen of Paul that urge us never to leave the side of our Lord.

Pray without ceasing. (1 Thess. 5:17 KJV)

Be constant in prayer. (Rom. 12:12 RSV)

Pray in the Spirit at all times. (Eph. 6:18)

Continue steadfastly in prayer. (Col. 4:2 RSV)

In everything . . . let your requests be made known to God. (Phil. 4:6 NASB)

Does unceasing communion seem daunting, complicated? Are you thinking, *Life is difficult enough. Why add this?* If so, remind yourself that God is the burden-remover, not the burden-giver. God intends that unceasing prayer lighten—not heighten—our load.

The more we search the Bible, the more we realize that unbroken communion with God is the intent and not the exception. Within the reach of *every* Christian is the unending presence of God.

PRACTICING THE PRESENCE

How, then, do I live in God's presence? How do I detect his unseen hand on my shoulder and his inaudible voice in my ear? A sheep grows familiar with the voice of the shepherd. How can you and I grow familiar with the voice of God? Here are a few ideas:

Give God your waking thoughts. Before you face the day, face the Father. Before you step out of bed, step into his presence. I have a friend who makes it a habit to roll out of his bed onto his knees and begin his day in prayer. Personally, I don't get that far. With my head still on the pillow and my eyes still closed, I offer God the first seconds of my day. The prayer is not lengthy and far from formal. Depending on how much sleep I got, it may not even be intelligible. Often it's nothing more than "Thank you for a night's rest. I belong to you today."

C. S. Lewis wrote: "The moment you wake up each morning . . . [all] your wishes and hopes for the day rush at you like wild animals. And the first job of each morning consists in shoving them all back; in listening to that other voice, taking that other point of view, letting that other, larger, stronger, quieter life come flowing in."⁵

Here is how the psalmist began his day: "Every morning, I tell you what I need, and I wait for your answer" (Ps. 5:3). Which leads to the second idea:

Give God your waiting thoughts. Spend time with him in silence. The mature married couple has learned the treasure of shared silence; they don't need to fill the air with constant chatter. Just being together is sufficient. Try being silent with God. "Be still, and know that I am God" (Ps. 46:10 NIV). Awareness of God is a fruit of stillness before God.

Dan Rather once asked Mother Teresa. "What do you say to God when you pray?"

Mother Teresa answered quietly, "I listen."

Taken aback, Rather tried again, "Well, then, what does God say?"

Mother Teresa smiled, "He listens."⁶

Give God your whispering thoughts. Through the centuries Christians have learned the value of brief sentence prayers, prayers that can be whispered anywhere, in any setting. Laubach sought unbroken communion with God by asking him questions. Every two or three minutes he would pray, "Am I in your will, Lord?" "Am I pleasing you, Lord?"

In the nineteenth century an anonymous Russian monk set out to live in unceasing communion with God. In a book entitled *The Way of the Pilgrim,* he tells of how he learned to have one prayer constantly in his mind: "Lord Jesus Christ, Son of God, have mercy on me, a sinner." With time, the prayer became so internalized that he was constantly praying it, even while consciously occupied with something else.

Imagine considering every moment as a potential time of communion with God. By the time your life is over, you will have spent six months at stoplights, eight months opening junk mail, a year and a half looking for lost stuff (double that number in my case), and a whopping five years standing in various lines.[7] Why don't you give these moments to God? By giving God your whispering thoughts, the common becomes uncommon. Simple phrases such as "Thank you, Father," "Be sovereign in this hour, O Lord," "You are my resting place, Jesus" can turn a commute into a pilgrimage. You needn't leave your office or kneel in your kitchen. Just pray where you are. Let the kitchen become a cathedral or the classroom a chapel. Give God your whispering thoughts.

And last, *give God your waning thoughts.* At the end of the day, let your mind settle on him. Conclude the day as you began it: talking to God. Thank him for the good parts. Question him about the hard parts. Seek his mercy. Seek his strength. And as you close your eyes, take assurance in the promise: "He who watches over Israel will neither slumber nor sleep" (Ps. 121:4 NIV). If you fall asleep as you pray, don't worry. What better place to doze off than in the arms of your Father.

Our faces, then, are not covered.
We all show the Lord's glory, and we are
being changed to be like him. This change
in us brings ever greater glory, which
comes from the Lord, who is the Spirit.

2 CORINTHIANS 3:18

Sunlight poured from his face.

MATTHEW 17:2 MSG

CHAPTER SIX

A Changed Face and a Set of Wings

A Worship-Hungry Heart

People on a plane and people on a pew have a lot in common. All are on a journey. Most are well-behaved and presentable. Some doze, and others gaze out the window. Most, if not all, are satisfied with a predictable experience. For many, the mark of a good flight and the mark of a good worship assembly are the same. "Nice," we like to say. "It was a nice flight/It was a nice worship service." We exit the same way we enter, and we're happy to return next time.

A few, however, are not content with nice. They long for something more. The boy who just passed me did. I heard him before I saw him. I was already in my seat when he asked, "Will they really let me meet the pilot?" He was either lucky or shrewd because he made the request just as he entered the plane. The question floated into the cockpit, causing the pilot to lean out.

"Someone looking for me?" he asked.

The boy's hand shot up like he was answering his second-grade teacher's question. "I am!"

"Well, come on in."

With a nod from his mom, the youngster entered the cockpit's world of controls and gauges and emerged minutes later with eyes wide. "Wow!" he exclaimed. "I'm so glad to be on this plane!"

No one else's face showed such wonder. I should know. I paid attention. The boy's interest piqued mine, so I studied the faces of the other passengers but found no such enthusiasm. I mostly saw contentment: travelers content to be on the plane, content to be closer to their destination, content to be out of the airport, content to sit and stare and say little.

There were a few exceptions. The five or so mid-age women wearing straw hats and carrying beachbags weren't content; they were exuberant. They giggled all the way down the aisle. My bet is they were moms-set-free-from-kitchens-and-kids. The fellow in the blue suit across the aisle wasn't content; he was cranky. He opened his laptop and scowled at its screen the entire trip. Most of us, however, were happier than he and more contained than the ladies. Most of us were content. Content with a predictable, uneventful flight. Content with a "nice" flight.

And since that is what we sought, that is what we got. The boy, on the other hand, wanted more. He wanted to see the pilot. If asked to describe the flight, he wouldn't say "nice." He'd likely produce the plastic wings the pilot gave him and say, "I saw the man up front."

Do you see why I say that people on a plane and people on

a pew have a lot in common? Enter a church sanctuary and look at the faces. A few are giggly, a couple are cranky, but by and large we are content. Content to be there. Content to sit and look straight ahead and leave when the service is over. Content to enjoy an assembly with no surprises or turbulence. Content with a "nice" service. "Seek and you will find," Jesus promised.[1] And since a nice service is what we seek, a nice service is usually what we find.

A few, however, seek more. A few come with the childlike enthusiasm of the boy. And those few leave as he did, wide-eyed with the wonder of having stood in the presence of the pilot himself.

COME ASKING

The same thing happened to Jesus. The day Jesus went to worship, his very face was changed.

"You're telling me that Jesus went to worship?"

I am. The Bible speaks of a day when Jesus took time to stand with friends in the presence of God. Let's read about the day Jesus went to worship:

> Six days later, Jesus took Peter, James, and John, the brother of James, up on a high mountain by themselves. While they watched, Jesus' appearance was changed; his face became bright like the sun, and his clothes became white as light. Then Moses and Elijah appeared to them, talking with Jesus.

Peter said to Jesus, "Lord, it is good that we are here. If you want, I will put up three tents here—one for you, one for Moses, and one for Elijah."

While Peter was talking, a bright cloud covered them. A voice came from the cloud and said, "This is my Son, whom I love, and I am very pleased with him. Listen to him!" (Matt. 17:1–5)

The words of Matthew presuppose a decision on the part of Jesus to stand in the presence of God. The simple fact that he chose his companions and went up on a mountain suggests this was no spur-of-the-moment action. He didn't awaken one morning, look at the calendar and then at his watch, and say, "Oops, today is the day we go to the mountain." No, he had preparations to make. Ministry to people was suspended so ministry to his heart could occur. Since his chosen place of worship was some distance away, he had to select the right path and stay on the right road. By the time he was on the mountain, his heart was ready. Jesus prepared for worship.

Let me ask you, do you do the same? Do you prepare for worship? What paths do you take to lead you up the mountain? The question may seem foreign, but my hunch is, many of us simply wake up and show up. We're sadly casual when it comes to meeting God.

Would we be so lackadaisical with, oh, let's say, the president? Suppose you were granted a Sunday morning breakfast at the White House? How would you spend Saturday night? Would you get ready? Would you collect your thoughts? Would you think about your questions and requests? Of course you would. Should we prepare any less for an encounter with the Holy God?

Let me urge you to come to worship prepared to worship. Pray before you come so you will be ready to pray when you arrive. Sleep before you come so you'll stay alert when you arrive. Read the Word before you come so your heart will be soft when you worship. Come hungry. Come willing. Come expecting God to speak. Come asking, even as you walk through the door, "Can I see the pilot today?"

REFLECTING HIS GLORY

As you do, you'll discover the purpose of worship—to change the face of the worshiper. This is exactly what happened to Christ on the mountain. Jesus' appearance was changed: "His face became bright like the sun" (Matt. 17:2).

The connection between the face and worship is more than coincidental. Our face is the most public part of our bodies, covered less than any other area. It is also the most recognizable part of our bodies. We don't fill a school annual with photos of people's feet but rather with photos of faces. God desires to take our faces, this exposed and memorable part of our bodies, and use them to reflect his goodness. Paul writes: "Our faces, then, are not covered. We all show the Lord's glory, and we are being changed to be like him. This change in us brings ever greater glory, which comes from the Lord, who is the Spirit" (2 Cor. 3:18).

God invites us to see his face so he can change ours. He uses our uncovered faces to display his glory. The transformation isn't easy. The sculptor of Mount Rushmore faced a lesser challenge than does God. But our Lord is up to the task. He loves to change the faces of his children. By his fingers, wrinkles of worry are rubbed away. Shadows of shame and doubt become portraits of grace and trust. He relaxes clenched jaws and smoothes furrowed brows. His touch can remove the bags of exhaustion from beneath the eyes and turn tears of despair into tears of peace.

How? Through worship.

We'd expect something more complicated, more demanding. A forty-day fast or the memorization of Leviticus perhaps. No. God's plan is simpler. He changes our faces through worship.

Exactly what is worship? I like King David's definition. "Oh magnify the LORD with me, and let us exalt His name together" (Ps. 34:3 NASB). Worship is the act of magnifying God. Enlarging our vision of him. Stepping into the cockpit to see where he sits and observe how he works. Of course, his size doesn't change, but our perception of him does. As we draw nearer, he seems larger. Isn't that what we need? A *big* view of God? Don't we have *big* problems, *big* worries, *big* questions? Of course we do. Hence we need a big view of God.

Worship offers that. How can we sing, "Holy, Holy, Holy" and not have our vision expanded? Or what about the lines from "It Is Well with My Soul"?

> My sin—O the bliss of this glorious thought,
> My sin—not in part but the whole,
> Is nailed to the cross and I bear it no more,
> Praise the Lord, praise the Lord, O my soul![2]

Can we sing those words and not have our countenance illuminated?

A vibrant, shining face is the mark of one who has stood in God's presence. After speaking to God, Moses had to cover his face with a veil (Exod. 34:33–35). After seeing heaven, Stephen's face glowed like that of an angel (Acts 6:15; 7:55–56).

God is in the business of changing the face of the world.

Let me be very clear. This change is his job, not ours. Our goal is not to make our faces radiant. Not even Jesus did that. Matthew says, "Jesus' appearance was changed" not "Jesus changed his appearance." Moses didn't even know his face was shining (Exod. 34:29). Our goal is not to conjure up some fake, frozen expression. Our goal is simply to stand before God with a prepared and willing heart and then let God do his work.

And he does. He wipes away the tears. He mops away the perspiration. He softens our furrowed brows. He touches our cheeks. He changes our faces as we worship.

But there's more. Not only does God change the face of those who worship, he changes those who watch us worship.

EVANGELISTIC WORSHIP

Remember the boy who went to see the pilot? His passion stirred me. I wanted to see the pilot, too. (And I wouldn't have refused the plastic wings.)

The same dynamic occurs when we come to worship with a heart of worship. Paul told the Corinthian church to worship in such a clear way that if an unbeliever entered, "he would find

. . . the secrets of his heart revealed; and . . . would fall down on his face and worship God, declaring that God is indeed among you" (1 Cor. 14:24–25 TJB).

David cites the evangelistic power of honest worship: "He put a new song in my mouth, a song of praise to our God. Many people will see this and worship him. Then they will trust the LORD" (Ps. 40:3).

Your heartfelt worship is a missionary appeal. Let unbelievers hear the passion of your voice or see the sincerity in your face, and they may be changed. Peter was. When Peter saw the worship of Jesus, he said, "Lord, it is good that we are here. If you want, I will put up three tents here—one for you, one for Moses, and one for Elijah" (Matt. 17:4).

Mark says Peter spoke out of fear (9:6). Luke says Peter spoke out of ignorance (9:33). But whatever the reason, at least Peter spoke. He wanted to do something for God. He didn't understand that God wants hearts and not tents, but at least he was moved to give something.

Why? Because he saw the transfigured face of Christ. The same happens in churches today. When people see us giving heartfelt praise to God—when they hear our worship—they are intrigued. They want to see the pilot! Sparks from our fire tend to ignite dry hearts.

I experienced something similar in Brazil. Our house was only blocks away from the largest soccer stadium in the world. At least once a week Maracana stadium would be packed with screaming soccer fans. Initially I was not numbered among them, but their enthusiasm was contagious. I wanted to see what they were so excited about. By the time I left Rio, I was a soccer convert and could shout with the rest of them.

Seekers may not understand all that happens in a house of worship. They may not understand the meaning of a song or the significance of the communion, but they know joy when they see it. And when they see your face changed, they may want to see God's face.

By the way, wouldn't the opposite be equally true? What happens when a seeker sees boredom on your face? Others are worshiping and you are scowling? Others are in his presence, but you are in your own little world? Others are seeking God's face while you are seeking the face of your wristwatch?

As long as I'm getting personal, may I come a step closer? Parents, what are your children learning from your worship? Do they see the same excitement as when you go to a basketball game? Do they see you prepare for worship as you do for a vacation? Do they see you hungry to arrive, seeking the face of the Father? Or do they see you content to leave the way you came?

They are watching. Believe me. They are watching.

Do you come to church with a worship-hungry heart? Our Savior did.

May I urge you to be just like Jesus? Prepare your heart for worship. Let God change your face through worship. Demonstrate the power of worship. Above all, seek the face of the pilot. The boy did. Because he sought the pilot, he left with a changed face and a set of wings. The same can happen to you.

*I ask—ask the God of our Master,
Jesus Christ, the God of glory—to make
you intelligent and discerning in knowing
him personally, your eyes focused and clear,
so that you can see exactly what it is
he is calling you to do.*

EPHESIANS 1:17–18 MSG

CHAPTER SEVEN

Golf Games
and Celery Sticks

A Focused Heart

The golf game was tied with four holes to go. As we stood on the tee box, I spotted the next green. "Sure seems like a long way off," I commented. No one spoke. "Sure is a narrow fairway," I said as I teed up my ball. Again, no response. "How do they expect us to hit over those trees?" Still no answer.

The silence didn't disturb me. Years of ruthless competition against fellow ministers on municipal courses has taught me to be wary of their tricks. I knew exactly what they were doing. Intimidated by my impressive streak of bogeys, they resolved to psych me out (after all, we were playing for a soda). So I stepped up to the ball and took a swing. There is no other way to describe what happened next—*I hit a great drive.* A high arching fade over the crop of trees to my left. I could hear the other guys groan. I assumed they were jealous. After watching their drives, I knew they were. None of them even made it close to the trees. Rather than hit left, they each hit right and ended up miles from the green. That's when I should have suspected something, but I didn't.

They walked down their side of the fairway, and I walked down mine. But rather than find my ball sitting up on thick fairway grass, I discovered it hidden in weeds and rocks and surrounded by trees. "This *is* a tough hole," I muttered to myself. Nevertheless, I was up for the challenge. I studied the shot and selected a strategy, took out a club, and—forgive me but I must say it again—*I hit a great shot*. You would have thought my ball was radar controlled: narrowly missing one branch, sweeping around another, heading toward the green like a jackrabbit dashing for supper. Only the steep hill kept it from rolling onto the putting surface.

I'd learned from televised tournaments how to act in such moments. I froze my follow-through just long enough for the photographers to take their pictures, then I gave my club a twirl. With one hand I waved to the crowd, with the other I handed my club to my caddie. Of course, in my case there was no photographer or caddie, and there was no crowd. Not even my buddies were watching. They were all on the other side of the fairway, looking in the other direction. A bit miffed that my skill had gone unnoticed, I shouldered my clubs and started walking to the green.

Again, it should have occurred to me that something was wrong. The tally of curious events should've gotten my attention. No one commenting on the difficulty of the hole. No one complimenting my drive. Everyone else hitting to the right while I hit to the left. A perfect drive landing in the rough. My splendid approach shot, unseen. It should have occurred to me, but it didn't. Only as I neared the green did anything seem unusual. Some players were already putting! Players I didn't know. Players whom I'd never seen before. Players who, I assumed, were either horribly slow or lost. I looked around for my group only to find them also on the green—on a *different* green.

That's when it hit me. I'd played the wrong hole! I had picked out the wrong target. I had thought we were playing to the green on the left when we were supposed to play to the green on the right! All of a sudden everything made sense. My buddies hit to the right because they were supposed to. The groan I heard after my drive was one of pity, not admiration. No wonder the hole seemed hard—I was playing in the wrong direction. How discouraging. Golf is tough enough as it is. It's even tougher when you're headed the wrong way.

THE HEART ON TARGET

The same can be said about life. Life is tough enough as it is. It's even tougher when we're headed in the wrong direction.

One of the incredible abilities of Jesus was to stay on target. His life never got off track. Not once do we find him walking down the wrong side of the fairway. He had no money, no computers, no jets, no administrative assistants or staff; yet Jesus did what many of us fail to do. He kept his life on course.

As Jesus looked across the horizon of his future, he could see many targets. Many flags were flapping in the wind, each of which he could have pursued. He could have been a political revolutionary. He could have been a national leader. He could have been content to be a teacher and educate minds or to be a physician and heal bodies. But in the end he chose to be a Savior and save souls.

Anyone near Christ for any length of time heard it from Jesus himself. "The Son of Man came to find lost people and save them" (Luke 19:10). "The Son of Man did not come to be served. He came to serve others and to give his life as a ransom for many people" (Mark 10:45).

The heart of Christ was relentlessly focused on one task. The day he left the carpentry shop of Nazareth he had one ultimate aim—the cross of Calvary. He was so focused that his final words were, "It is finished" (John 19:30).

How could Jesus say he was finished? There were still the hungry to feed, the sick to heal, the untaught to instruct, and the unloved to love. How could he say he was finished? Simple. He had completed his designated task. His commission was fulfilled. The painter could set aside his brush, the sculptor lay down his chisel, the writer put away his pen. The job was done.

Wouldn't you love to be able to say the same? Wouldn't you love to look back on your life and know you had done what you were called to do?

DISTRACTED HEARTS

Our lives tend to be so scattered. Intrigued by one trend only until the next comes along. Suckers for the latest craze or quick fix. This project, then another. Lives with no strategy, no goal, no defining priority. Playing the holes out of order. Erratic. Hesitant. Living life with the hiccups. We are easily distracted by the small things and forget the big things. I saw an example of this the other day in the grocery store.

There is one section in the supermarket where I am a seasoned veteran: the sample section. I'm never one to pass up a snack. Last Saturday I went to the back of the store where the samplers tend to linger. Bingo! There were two sample givers awaiting hungry sample takers. One had a skillet of sausage and the other a plate full of cream-cheese-covered celery. You'll be proud to know I opted for the celery. I wanted the sausage, but I knew the celery was better for me.

Unfortunately, the celery lady never saw me. She was too busy straightening her sticks. I walked past her, and she never looked up. The sausage lady, however, saw me coming and extended the plate. I declined and made another circle past the celery lady. Same response. She never saw me. She was too busy getting her plate in order. So I made another loop past the sausage lady. Once again the offer came, and once again—with admirable resolve, I might add—I resisted. I was committed to doing the right thing.

So was the celery lady. She was determined to get every celery stick just so on her plate. But she cared more about the appearance of her product than the distribution. I stopped. I coughed. I cleared my throat. I did everything but sing a song. Still no response. The sausage lady, however, was waiting on me with sizzling sausage. I gave in; I ate the sausage.

The celery lady made the same mistake I had made on the golf course. She got off target. She was so occupied with the small matters (i.e., celery organization) that she forgot her assignment (i.e., to help needy, hungry, pitiful shoppers like me).

How do we keep from making the same mistake in life? God wants us to be just like Jesus and have focused hearts. How do I select the right flag and stay on target? Consulting the map would be a good start. I would have saved myself a lot of hassle that day had I taken enough time to look at the map on the scorecard. The course architect had drawn one. What's true on the golf course is true in life as well. The one who designed our course left us directions. By answering four simple questions, we can be more like Jesus; we can stay on course with our lives.

AM I FITTING INTO GOD'S PLAN?

Romans 8:28 says, "We know that all that happens to us is working for our good if we love God and are fitting into his plans" (TLB). The first step for focusing your heart is to ask this question: Am I fitting into God's plan?

God's plan is to save his children. "He does not want any-one to be destroyed but wants all to turn away from their sins" (2 Pet. 3:9 TEV).

If God's goal is the salvation of the world, then my goal should be the same. The details will differ from person to person, but the big picture is identical for all of us. "We're Christ's representatives. God uses us to persuade men and women" (2 Cor. 5:20 MSG). Regardless of what you don't know about

your future, one thing is certain: you are intended to contribute to the good plan of God, to tell others about the God
who loves them and longs to bring them home.

But exactly how are you to contribute? What is your specific
assignment? Let's seek the answer with a second question.

WHAT ARE MY LONGINGS?

This question may surprise you. Perhaps you thought your
longings had nothing to do with keeping your life on track. I
couldn't disagree more. Your heart is crucial. Psalm 37:4 says,
"Enjoy serving the LORD, and he will give you what you want."
When we submit to God's plans, we can trust our desires. Our
assignment is found at the intersection of God's plan and our
pleasures. *What do you love to do? What brings you joy? What gives
you a sense of satisfaction?*

Some long to feed the poor. Others enjoy leading the
church. Others relish singing or teaching or holding the hands
of the sick or counseling the confused. Each of us has been
made to serve God in a unique way.

"We are God's workmanship, created in Christ Jesus to do
good works, which God prepared in advance for us to do"
(Eph. 2:10 NIV).

"You made all the delicate, inner parts of my body, and knit
them together in my mother's womb. . . . Your workmanship is
marvelous. . . . You were there while I was being formed. . . .
You saw me before I was born and scheduled each day of my life
before I began to breathe" (Ps. 139:13–16 TLB).

You are a custom design; you are tailor-made. God prescribed your birth. Regardless of the circumstances that surrounded your arrival, you are not an accident. God planned you before you were born.

The longings of your heart, then, are not incidental; they are critical messages. The desires of your heart are not to be ignored; they are to be consulted. As the wind turns the weather vane, so God uses your passions to turn your life. God is too gracious to ask you to do something you hate.

Be careful, however. Don't consider your desires without considering your skills. Move quickly to the third question.

WHAT ARE MY ABILITIES?

There are some things we want to do but simply aren't equipped to accomplish. I, for example, have the desire to sing. Singing for others would give me wonderful satisfaction. The problem is, it wouldn't give the same satisfaction to my audience. I am what you might call a prison singer—I never have the key, and I'm always behind a few bars.

Paul gives good advice in Romans 12:3: "Have a sane estimate of your capabilities" (PHILLIPS).

In other words, be aware of your strengths. When you teach, do people listen? When you lead, do people follow? When you administer, do things improve? Where are you most productive? Identify your strengths, and then—this is important—major in them. Take a few irons out of the fire so this one can get hot. Failing to focus on our strengths may prevent us from accomplishing the unique tasks God has called us to do.

A lighthouse keeper who worked on a rocky stretch of coastline received oil once a month to keep his light burning. Not being far from a village, he had frequent guests. One night a woman needed oil to keep her family warm. Another night a father needed oil for his lamp. Then another needed oil to lubricate a wheel. All the requests seemed legitimate, so the lighthouse keeper tried to meet them all. Toward the end of the month, however, he ran out of oil, and his lighthouse went dark, causing several ships to crash on the coastline. The man was reproved by his superiors, "You were given the oil for one reason," they said, "to keep the light burning."[1]

We cannot meet every need in the world. We cannot please every person in the world. We cannot satisfy every request in the world. But some of us try. And in the end, we run out of fuel. Have a sane estimate of your abilities and stick to them.

One final question is needed.

AM I SERVING GOD NOW?

Upon reading this, you may start feeling restless. *Maybe I need to change jobs. Perhaps I should relocate. I guess Max is telling me I need to go to seminary* . . . No, not necessarily.

Again, Jesus is the ideal example. When do we get our first clue that he knows he is the Son of God? In the temple of Jerusalem. He is twelve years old. His parents are three days into the return trip to Nazareth before they notice he is missing.

They find him in the temple studying with the leaders. When they ask him for an explanation, he says, "Did you not know that I must be about My Father's business" (Luke 2:49 NKJV).

As a young boy, Jesus already senses the call of God. But what does he do next? Recruit apostles and preach sermons and perform miracles? No, he goes home to his folks and learns the family business.

That is exactly what you should do. Want to bring focus to your life? Do what Jesus did. Go home, love your family, and take care of business. *But Max, I want to be a missionary.* Your first mission field is under your roof. What makes you think they'll believe you overseas if they don't believe you across the hall?

But Max, I'm ready to do great things for God. Good, do them at work. Be a good employee. Show up on time with a good attitude. Don't complain or grumble, but "work as if you were doing it for the Lord, not for people" (Col. 3:23).

THE P.L.A.N.

Pretty simple plan, don't you think? It's even easy to remember. Perhaps you caught the acrostic:

> Am I fitting into God's **P**lan?
> What are my **L**ongings?
> What are my **A**bilities?
> Am I serving God **N**ow?

Why don't you take a few moments and evaluate your direction? Ask yourself the four questions. You may find that you are doing what I did: hitting some good shots but in the wrong direction. In my case it cost me three sodas. I lost so many strokes I never caught up.

The same needn't be said about you, however. God allows you to start fresh at any point in life. "From now on, then, you must live the rest of your earthly lives controlled by God's will and not by human desires" (1 Pet. 4:2 TEV).

Circle the words *from now on*. God will give you a fresh scorecard. Regardless of what has controlled you in the past, it's never too late to get your life on course and be a part of God's P.L.A.N.

So from now on,
there must be no more lies.
Speak the truth to one another.

EPHESIANS 4:25 TJB

CHAPTER EIGHT

❧✦❧

NOTHING BUT THE TRUTH

An Honest Heart

A woman stands before judge and jury, places one hand on the Bible and the other in the air, and makes a pledge. For the next few minutes, with God as her helper, she will "tell the truth, the whole truth, and nothing but the truth."

She is a witness. Her job is not to expand upon nor dilute the truth. Her job is to tell the truth. Leave it to the legal counsel to interpret. Leave it to the jury to resolve. Leave it to the judge to apply. But the witness? The witness speaks the truth. Let her do more or less and she taints the outcome. But let her do that—let her tell the truth—and justice has a chance.

The Christian, too, is a witness. We, too, make a pledge. Like the witness in court, we are called to tell the truth. The bench may be absent and the judge unseen, but the Bible is present, the watching world is the jury, and we are the primary witnesses. We are subpoenaed by no less than Jesus himself: "You

---

will be my *witnesses*—in Jerusalem, in all of Judea, in Samaria, and in every part of the world" (Acts 1:8, italics mine).

We are witnesses. And like witnesses in a court, we are called to testify, to tell what we have seen and heard. And we are to speak truthfully. Our task is not to whitewash nor bloat the truth. Our task is to tell the truth. Period.

There is, however, one difference between the witness in court and the witness for Christ. The witness in court eventually steps down from the witness chair, but the witness for Christ never does. Since the claims of Christ are always on trial, court is perpetually in session, and we remain under oath. For the Christian, deception is never an option. It wasn't an option for Jesus.

WHAT GOD CAN'T DO

One of the most astounding assessments of Christ is this summary: "He had done nothing wrong, and he had never lied" (Isa. 53:9). Jesus was staunchly honest. His every word accurate, his every sentence true. No cheating on tests. No altering the accounts. Not once did Jesus stretch the truth. Not once did he shade the truth. Not once did he avoid the truth. He simply told the truth. No deceit was found in his mouth.

And if God has his way with us, none will be found in ours. He longs for us to be just like Jesus. His plan, if you remember, is to shape us along the lines of his Son (Rom. 8:28). He seeks not to decrease or minimize our deception but to eliminate our deception. God is blunt about dishonesty: "No one who is dishonest will live in my house" (Ps. 101:7).

Our Master has a strict honor code. From Genesis to Revelation, the theme is the same: God loves the truth and hates deceit. In 1 Corinthians 6:9–10 Paul lists the type of people who will not inherit the kingdom of God. The covey he portrays is a ragged assortment of those who sin sexually, worship idols, take part in adultery, sell their bodies, get drunk, rob people, and—there it is—*lie about others.*

Such rigor may surprise you. *You mean my fibbing and flattering stir the same heavenly anger as adultery and aggravated assault?* Apparently so. God views fudging on income tax the same way he views kneeling before idols.

> The LORD hates those who tell lies but is pleased with those who keep their promises. (Prov. 12:22)
>
> The LORD hates . . . a lying tongue. (Prov. 6:16–17)
>
> [God] destroys liars . . . [and] hates those who kill and trick others. (Ps. 5:6)

Why? Why the hard line? Why the tough stance?

For one reason: dishonesty is absolutely contrary to the character of God. According to Hebrews 6:18, *it is impossible for God to lie.* It's not that God will not lie or that he has chosen not to lie—*he cannot lie.* For God to lie is for a dog to fly and a bird to bark. It simply cannot happen. The Book of Titus echoes the same three words as the Book of Hebrews: "God cannot lie" (Titus 1:2).

God always speaks truth. When he makes a covenant, he keeps it. When he makes a statement, he means it. And when he proclaims the truth, we can believe it. What he says is true. Even "if we are not faithful, [God] will still be faithful, because he cannot be false to himself" (2 Tim. 2:13).

Satan, on the other hand, finds it impossible to tell the truth. According to Jesus, the devil is "the father of lies" (John 8:44). If you'll remember, deceit was the first tool out of the devil's bag. In the Garden of Eden, Satan didn't discourage Eve. He didn't seduce her. He didn't sneak up on her. He just lied to her. "God says you'll die if you eat the fruit? You will not die" (see Gen. 3:1–4).

BIG FAT LIAR. But Eve was suckered, and the fruit was plucked, and it's not more than a few paragraphs before husband and son are following suit and the honesty of Eden seems a distant memory.

It still does. Daniel Webster was right when he observed, "There is nothing as powerful as the truth and often nothing as strange."

THE WAGES OF DECEIT

According to a *Psychology Today* survey, the devil is still spinning webs, and we are still plucking fruit.

- More people say they have cheated on their marriage partners than on their tax returns or expense accounts.

- More than half say that if their tax returns were audited, they would probably owe the government money.

- About one out of three people admits to deceiving a best friend about something within the last year; 96 percent of them feel guilty about it.

- Nearly half predict that if they scratched another car in the parking lot, they would drive away without leaving a note—although the vast majority (89 percent) agree that would be immoral.[1]

Perhaps the question shouldn't be "Why does God demand such honesty?" but rather "Why do we tolerate such dishonesty?" Never was Jeremiah more the prophet than when he announced: "The heart is deceitful above all things" (Jer. 17:9 NIV). How do we explain our dishonesty? What's the reason for our forked tongues and greasy promises? We don't need a survey to find the answer.

For one thing, we don't like the truth. Most of us can sympathize with the fellow who received a call from his wife just as she was about to fly home from Europe. "How's my cat?" she asked.

"Dead."

"Oh, honey, don't be so honest. Why didn't you break the news to me slowly? You've ruined my trip."

"What do you mean?"

"You could have told me he was on the roof. And when I called you from Paris, you could have told me he was acting sluggish. Then when I called from London, you could have said he was sick, and when I called you from New York, you could have said he was at the vet. Then, when I arrived home, you could have said he was dead."

The husband had never been exposed to such protocol but was willing to learn. "OK," he said. "I'll do better next time."

"By the way," she asked, "how's Mom?"

There was a long silence, then he replied, "Uh, she's on the roof."

The plain fact is we don't like the truth. Our credo is *You shall know the truth, and the truth shall make you squirm.* Our dislike for the truth began at the age of three when mom walked into our rooms and asked, "Did you hit your little brother?" We knew then and there that honesty had its consequences. So we learned to, uhhh, well, it's not *really* lying . . . we learned to cover things up.

"Did I hit baby brother? That all depends on how you interpret the word *hit*. I mean, sure I made contact with him, but would a jury consider it a 'hit'? Everything is relative, you know."

"Did I hit baby brother? Yes, Dad, I did. But it's not my fault. Had I been born with nonaggressive chromosomes, and had you not permitted me to watch television, it never would have happened. So, you can say I hit my brother, but the fault isn't mine. I'm a victim of nurture and nature."

The truth, we learn early, is not fun. We don't like the truth.

Not only do we not like the truth, *we don't trust the truth*. If we are brutally honest (which is advisable in a discussion on honesty), we'd have to admit that the truth seems inadequate to do what we need done.

We want our bosses to like us, so we flatter. We call it polishing the apple. God calls it a lie.

We want people to admire us, so we exaggerate. We call it stretching the truth. God calls it a lie.

We want people to respect us, so we live in houses we can't afford and charge bills we can't pay. We call it the American way. God calls it living a lie.

IF WE DON'T TELL THE TRUTH

Ananias and Sapphira represent just how much we humans do not trust the truth. They sold a piece of property and gave half the money to the church. They lied to Peter and the apostles, claiming that the land sold for the amount they gave. Their sin was not in holding back some of the money for themselves; it was in misrepresenting the truth. Their deceit resulted in their deaths. Luke writes: "The whole church and all the others who heard about these things were filled with fear" (Acts 5:11).

More than once I've heard people refer to this story with a nervous chuckle and say, "I'm glad God doesn't still strike people dead for lying." I'm not so sure he doesn't. It seems to me that the wages of deceit is still death. Not death of the body, perhaps, but the death of:

- *a marriage*—Falsehoods are termites in the trunk of the family tree.

- *a conscience*—The tragedy of the second lie is that it is always easier to tell than the first.

- *a career*—Just ask the student who got booted out for cheating or the employee who got fired for embezzlement if the lie wasn't fatal.

- *faith*—The language of faith and the language of falsehood have two different vocabularies. Those fluent in the language of falsehood find terms like *confession* and *repentance* hard to pronounce.

We could also list the deaths of intimacy, trust, peace, credibility, and self-respect. But perhaps the most tragic death that occurs from deceit is our witness. The court won't listen to the testimony of a perjured witness. Neither will the world. Do we think our coworkers will believe our words about Christ when they can't even believe our words about how we handled our expense account? Even more significantly, do we think God will use us as a witness if we won't tell the truth?

Every high school football team has a player whose assignment is to carry the play from the coach to the huddle. What if the player doesn't tell the truth? What if the coach calls for a pass but the courier says the coach called for a run? One thing is certain: the coach won't call on that player very long. God says if we are faithful with the small things, he'll trust us with the greater things (Matt. 25:21). Can he trust you with the small things?

FACING THE MUSIC

Many years ago a man conned his way into the orchestra of the emperor of China although he could not play a note. Whenever the group practiced or performed, he would hold his flute against his lips, pretending to play but not making a sound. He received a modest salary and enjoyed a comfortable living.

Then one day the emperor requested a solo from each musician. The flutist got nervous. There wasn't enough time to learn the instrument. He pretended to be sick, but the royal physician wasn't fooled. On the day of his solo performance, the impostor took poison and killed himself. The explanation of his suicide led to a phrase that found its way into the English language: "He refused to face the music."[2]

The cure for deceit is simply this: face the music. Tell the truth. Some of us are living in deceit. Some of us are walking in the shadows. The lies of Ananias and Sapphira resulted in death; so have ours. Some of us have buried a marriage, parts of a conscience, and even parts of our faith—all because we won't tell the truth.

Are you in a dilemma, wondering if you should tell the truth or not? The question to ask in such moments is, Will God bless my deceit? Will he, who hates lies, bless a strategy built on lies? Will the Lord, who loves the truth, bless the business of falsehoods? Will God honor the career of the manipulator? Will God come to the aid of the cheater? Will God bless my dishonesty?

I don't think so either.

Examine your heart. Ask yourself some tough questions.

Am I being completely honest with my spouse and children? Are my relationships marked by candor? What about my work or school environment? Am I honest in my dealings? Am I a trustworthy student? An honest taxpayer? A reliable witness at work?

Do you tell the truth . . . always?

If not, start today. Don't wait until tomorrow. The ripple of today's lie is tomorrow's wave and next year's flood. Start today. Be just like Jesus. Tell the truth, the whole truth, and nothing but the truth.

Be self-controlled and alert.
Your enemy the devil prowls around like a
roaring lion looking for someone to devour.
Resist him, standing firm in the faith.

1 PETER 5:8–9 NIV

CHAPTER NINE

THE GREENHOUSE
OF THE MIND

A Pure Heart

Suppose you come to visit me one day and find me working in my green-house. (Neither my house nor thumb is green, but let's pre-tend.) I explain to you that the greenhouse was a gift from my father. He used state-of-the-art equipment to create the ideal structure for growth. The atmosphere is perfect. The lighting exact. The temperature is suited for flowers, fruit, or anything I want, and what I want is flowers and fruit.

I ask you to join me as I collect some seeds to plant. You've always thought I was a bit crazy, but what I do next removes all doubt. You watch me walk into a field and strip seeds off of weeds. Crab grass seeds, dandelion seeds, grass burr seeds. I fill a bag with a variety of weed seeds and return to the greenhouse.

You can't believe what you've just seen. "I thought you wanted a greenhouse full of flowers and fruit."

"I do."

"Then don't you think you ought to plant flower seeds and fruit seeds?"

"Do you have any idea how much those seeds cost? Besides, you have to drive all the way to the garden center to get them. No thanks, I'm taking the cheap and easy route."

You walk away mumbling something about one brick short of a load.

THE GREENHOUSE OF THE HEART

Everybody knows you harvest what you sow. You reap what you plant. Yet strangely, what we know when we develop land, we tend to forget when we cultivate our hearts.

Think for a moment of your heart as a greenhouse. The similarities come quickly. It, too, is a magnificent gift from your father. It, too, is perfectly suited for growing. And your heart, like a greenhouse, has to be managed.

Consider for a moment your thoughts as seed. Some thoughts become flowers. Others become weeds. Sow seeds of hope and enjoy optimism. Sow seeds of doubt and expect insecurity. "People harvest only what they plant" (Gal. 6:7).

The proof is everywhere you look. Ever wonder why some people have the Teflon capacity to resist negativism and remain patient, optimistic, and forgiving? Could it be that they have diligently sown seeds of goodness and are enjoying the harvest?

Ever wonder why others have such a sour outlook? Such a gloomy attitude? You would, too, if your heart were a greenhouse of weeds and thorns.

Perhaps you've heard the joke about the man who came home one day to a cranky wife. Arriving at 6:30 in the evening, he spent an hour trying to cheer her up. Nothing worked. Finally he said, "Let's start over and pretend I'm just getting home." He stepped outside, and when he opened the door, she said, "It's 7:30, and you're just now getting home from work?"

The wife was reaping the harvest of a few weedy thoughts. Let's pause and make an important application. If the heart is a greenhouse and our thoughts are seeds, shouldn't we be careful about what we sow? Shouldn't we be selective about the seeds we allow to come into the greenhouse? Shouldn't there be a sentry at the door? Isn't guarding the heart a strategic task? According to the Bible it is: "Above all else, guard your heart, for it is the wellspring of life" (Prov. 4:23 NIV). Or as another translation reads: "Be careful what you think, because your thoughts run your life."

What a true statement! Test the principle, and see if you don't agree.

Two drivers are stuck in the same traffic jam. One person stews in anger, thinking, *My schedule is messed up.* The other sighs in relief, *Good chance to slow down.*

Two mothers face the same tragedy. One is destroyed: *I'll never get over this.* The other is despondent but determined: *God will get me through.*

Two executives face the same success. One pats himself on the back and grows cocky. The other gives the credit to God and grows grateful.

Two husbands commit the same failure. One bitterly assumes

God's limit of grace has been crossed. The other gratefully assumes a new depth of God's grace has been discovered.

"Above all else, guard your heart, for it is the wellspring of life."

Let's look at it from another angle. Suppose I ask you to take care of my house while I'm out of town. You pledge to keep everything in great shape. But when I return, I find the place in shambles. The carpet is torn, walls are smeared, furniture is broken. Your explanation is not impressive: some bikers came by and needed a place to stay. Then the rugby team called, looking for a place for their party. And of course there was the fraternity—they wanted a place to hold their initiation ceremony. As the owner, I have one question: "Don't you know how to say no? This is not your house. You don't have the right to let in everyone who wants to enter."

Ever think God wants to say the same to us?

GUARDING OUR HEARTS

You've got to admit some of our hearts are trashed out. Let any riffraff knock on the door, and we throw it open. Anger shows up, and we let him in. Revenge needs a place to stay, so we have him pull up a chair. Pity wants to have a party, so we show him the kitchen. Lust rings the bell, and we change the sheets on the bed. Don't we know how to say no?

Many don't. For most of us, thought management is, well, unthought of. We think much about time management, weight management, personnel management, even scalp management.

But what about thought management? Shouldn't we be as concerned about managing our thoughts as we are managing anything else? Jesus was. Like a trained soldier at the gate of a city, he stood watch over his mind. He stubbornly guarded the gateway of his heart. Many thoughts were denied entrance. Need a few examples?

How about arrogance? On one occasion the people determined to make Jesus their king. What an attractive thought. Most of us would delight in the notion of royalty. Even if we refused the crown, we would enjoy considering the invitation. Not Jesus. "Jesus saw that in their enthusiasm, they were about to grab him and make him king, so he slipped off and went back up the mountain to be by himself" (John 6:15 MSG).

Another dramatic example occurred in a conversation Jesus had with Peter. Upon hearing Jesus announce his impending death on the cross, the impetuous apostle objected. "Impossible, Master! That can never be!" (Matt. 16:22 MSG). Apparently, Peter was about to question the necessity of Calvary. But he never had a chance. Christ blocked the doorway. He sent both the messenger and the author of the heresy scurrying: "Peter, get out of my way. Satan, get lost. You have no idea how God works" (Matt. 16:23 MSG).

And how about the time Jesus was mocked? Have you ever had people laugh at you? Jesus did, too. Responding to an appeal to heal a sick girl, he entered her house only to be told she was dead. His response? "The child is not dead but sleeping." The response of the people in the house? "They laughed at him." Just like all of us, Jesus had to face a moment of humiliation. But unlike most of us, he refused to receive it. Note his decisive response: "he put them all outside" (Mark 5:39–40 RSV). The mockery was not allowed in the house of the girl nor in the mind of Christ.

Jesus guarded his heart. If he did, shouldn't we do the same? Most certainly! "Be careful what you think, because your thoughts run your life" (Prov. 4:23). Jesus wants your heart to be fertile and fruitful. He wants you to have a heart like his. That is God's goal for you. He wants you to "think and act like Christ Jesus" (Phil. 2:5). But how? The answer is surprisingly simple. We can be transformed if we make one decision: *I will submit my thoughts to the authority of Jesus.*

It's easy to overlook a significant claim made by Christ at the conclusion of Matthew's gospel. "All authority in heaven and on earth has been given to me" (Matt. 28:18 NIV). Jesus claims to be the CEO of heaven and earth. He has the ultimate say on everything, especially our thoughts. He has more authority, for example, than your parents. Your parents may say you are no good, but Jesus says you are valuable, and he has authority over parents. He even has more authority over you than you do. You may tell yourself that you are too bad to be forgiven, but Jesus has a different opinion. If you give him authority over you, then your guilty thoughts are no longer allowed.

Jesus also has authority over your ideas. Suppose you have an idea that you want to rob a grocery store. Jesus, however, has made it clear that stealing is wrong. If you have given him authority over your ideas, then the idea of stealing cannot remain in your thoughts.

See what I mean by authority? To have a pure heart, we must submit all thoughts to the authority of Christ. If we are willing to do that, he will change us to be like him. Here is how it works.

GUARD AT THE DOORWAY

Let's return to the image of the greenhouse. Your heart is a fertile greenhouse ready to produce good fruit. Your mind is the doorway to your heart—the strategic place where you determine which seeds are sown and which seeds are discarded. The Holy Spirit is ready to help you manage and filter the thoughts that try to enter. He can help you guard your heart.

He stands with you on the threshold. A thought approaches, a questionable thought. Do you throw open the door and let it enter? Of course not. You "fight to capture every thought until it acknowledges the authority of Christ" (2 Cor. 10:5 PHILLIPS). You don't leave the door unguarded. You stand equipped with handcuffs and leg irons, ready to capture any thought not fit to enter.

For the sake of discussion, let's say a thought regarding your personal value approaches. With all the cockiness of a neighborhood bully, the thought swaggers up to the door and says, "You're a loser. All your life you've been a loser. You've blown relationships and jobs and ambitions. You might as well write the word *bum* on your résumé, for that is what you are."

The ordinary person would throw open the door and let the thought in. Like a seed from a weed, it would find fertile soil and take root and bear thorns of inferiority. The average person would say, "You're right. I'm a bum. Come on in."

But as a Christian, you aren't your average person. You are led by the Spirit. So rather than let the thought in, you take it captive. You handcuff it and march it down the street to the courthouse where you present the thought before the judgment seat of Christ.

"Jesus, this thought says I'm a bum and a loser and that I'll never amount to anything. What do you think?"

See what you are doing? You are submitting the thought to the authority of Jesus. If Jesus agrees with the thought, then let it in. If not, kick it out. In this case Jesus disagrees.

How do know if Jesus agrees or disagrees? You open your Bible. What does God think about you? Ephesians 2:10 is a good place to check: "For we are God's workmanship, created in Christ Jesus to do good works, which God prepared in advance for us to do" (NIV). Or how about Romans 8:1: "There is now no condemnation for those who are in Christ Jesus" (NIV)?

Obviously any thought that says you are inferior or insignificant does not pass the test—and does not gain entrance. You have the right to give the bully a firm kick in the pants and watch him run.

Let's take another example. The first thought was a bully; this next thought is a groupie. She comes not to tell you how bad you are but how good you are. She rushes to the doorway and gushes, "You are so good. You are so wonderful. The world is so lucky to have you," and on and on the groupie grovels.

Typically this is the type of thought you'd welcome. But you don't do things the typical way. You guard your heart. You walk in the Spirit. And you take every thought captive. So once again you go to Jesus. You submit this thought to the authority of Christ. As you unsheathe the sword of the Spirit, his Word, you learn that pride doesn't please God.

"Don't cherish exaggerated ideas of yourself or your importance" (Rom. 12:3 PHILLIPS).

"The cross of our Lord Jesus Christ is my only reason for bragging" (Gal. 6:14).

As much as you'd like to welcome this thought of conceit into the greenhouse, you can't. You only allow what Christ allows.

One more example. This time the thought is not one of criticism or flattery but one of temptation. If you're a fellow, the thought is dressed in flashy red. If you're a female, the thought is the hunk you've always wanted. There is the brush of the hand, the fragrance in the air, and the invitation. "Come on, it's all right. We're consenting adults."

What do you do? Well, if you aren't under the authority of Christ, you throw open the door. But if you have the mind of Christ, you step back and say, "Not so fast. You'll have to get permission from my big brother." So you take this steamy act before Jesus and ask, "Yes or no?"

Nowhere does he answer more clearly than in 1 Corinthians 6 and 7: "We must not pursue the kind of sex that avoids commitment and intimacy, leaving us more lonely than ever. . . . Is it a good thing to have sexual relations? Certainly—but only within a certain context. It's good for a man to have a wife, and for a woman to have a husband. Sexual drives are strong, but marriage is strong enough to contain them" (6:18; 7:1–2 MSG).

Now armed with the opinion of Christ and the sword of the Spirit, what do you do? Well, if the tempter is not your spouse, close the door. If the invitation is from your spouse, then HUBBA HUBBA HUBBA.

The point is this. Guard the doorway of your heart. Submit your thoughts to the authority of Christ. The more selective you are about seeds, the more delighted you will be with the crop.

Let your hope keep you joyful,
be patient in your troubles,
and pray at all times.

ROMANS 12:12 TEV

CHAPTER TEN

FINDING GOLD
IN THE GARBAGE

A Hope-Filled Heart

William Rathje likes garbage. This Harvard-educated researcher is convinced we can learn a lot from the trash dumps of the world. Archaeologists have always examined trash to study a society. Rathje does the same; he just eliminates the wait. The Garbage Project, as he calls his organization, travels across the continent, excavating landfills and documenting our eating habits, dress styles, and economic levels.[1] Rathje is able to find meaning in our garbage.

His organization documented that the average household wastes 10 percent to 15 percent of its solid food. The average American produces half a pound of trash per day, and the largest landfill in America, located near New York City, has enough trash to fill the Panama Canal. According to Rathje, trash decomposes more slowly than we thought it did. He found a whole steak from 1973 and readable newspapers from the Truman presidency. Rathje learns a lot by looking at our junk.

Reading about Rathje made me wonder, *What is it like to be a "garbologist"?* When he gives a speech, is the address referred to as "trash talk"? Are his staff meetings designated as "rubbish reviews"? Are his business trips called "junkets"? When he day-dreams about his work, does his wife tell him to get his mind out of the garbage?

Though I prefer to leave the dirty work to Rathje, his attitude toward trash intrigues me. What if we learned to do the same? Suppose we changed the way we view the garbage that comes our way? After all, don't you endure your share of rubbish? Snarled traffic. Computer foul-ups. Postponed vacations.

And then there are the days that a Dumpster couldn't hold all the garbage we face: hospital bills, divorce papers, pay cuts, and betrayals. What do you do when an entire truck of sorrow is dumped on you?

On Rathje's office wall is a framed headline he found in a paper: "Gold in Garbage." This garbologist finds treasure in trash. Jesus did the same. What everyone else perceived as calamity, he saw as opportunity. And because he saw what others didn't, he found what others missed.

Early in his ministry Jesus said this about our vision: "Your eyes are windows into your body. If you open your eyes wide in wonder and belief, your body fills up with light. If you live squinty-eyed in greed and distrust, your body is a dank cellar" (Matt. 6:22–23 MSG).

In other words, how we look at life determines how we live

life. But Jesus did much more than articulate this principle, he modeled it.

THE DARKEST NIGHT IN HISTORY

On the night before his death, a veritable landfill of woes tumbled in on Jesus. Somewhere between the Gethsemane prayer and the mock trial is what has to be the darkest scene in the history of the human drama. Though the entire episode couldn't have totaled more than five minutes, the event had enough badness to fill a thousand Dumpsters. Except for Christ, not one person did one good thing. Search the scene for an ounce of courage or a speck of character, and you won't find it. What you will find is a compost heap of deceit and betrayal. Yet in it all, Jesus saw reason to hope. And in his outlook, we find an example to follow.

"Get up, we must go. Look, here comes the man who has turned against me."

While Jesus was still speaking, Judas, one of the twelve apostles, came up. With him were many people carrying swords and clubs who had been sent from the leading priests and the older Jewish leaders of the people. Judas had planned to give them a signal, saying, "The man I kiss is Jesus. Arrest him." At once Judas went to Jesus and said, "Greetings, Teacher!" and kissed him.

Jesus answered, "Friend, do what you came to do."

Then the people came and grabbed Jesus and arrested

him. When that happened, one of Jesus' followers reached for his sword and pulled it out. He struck the servant of the high priest and cut off his ear.

Jesus said to the man, "Put your sword back in its place. All who use swords will be killed with swords. Surely you know I could ask my Father, and he would give me more than twelve armies of angels. But it must happen this way to bring about what the Scriptures say."

Then Jesus said to the crowd, "You came to get me with swords and clubs as if I were a criminal. Every day I sat in the Temple teaching, and you did not arrest me there. But all these things have happened so that it will come about as the prophets wrote." Then all of Jesus' followers left him and ran away (Matt. 26:46–56).

Had a reporter been assigned to cover the arrest, his head-line might have read:

A DARK NIGHT FOR JESUS
Galilean Preacher Abandoned by Friends

Last Friday they welcomed him with palm leaves. Last night they arrested him with swords. The world of Jesus of Nazareth turned sour as he was apprehended by a crowd of soldiers and angry citizens in a garden just out-side the city walls. Only a week since his triumphant entry, his popularity has taken a fatal plunge. Even his fol-lowers refuse to claim him. The disciples who took pride in being seen with him earlier in the week took flight from him last night. With the public crying for his death and the disciples denying any involvement, the future of this celebrated teacher appears bleak, and the impact of his mission appears limited.

The darkest night of Jesus' life was marked by one crisis after another. In just a moment we will see what Jesus saw, but first let's consider what an observer would have witnessed in the Garden of Gethsemane.

First he would have seen *unanswered prayer*. Jesus had just offered an anguished appeal to God. "My Father, if it is possible, do not give me this cup of suffering. But do what you want, not what I want" (26:39). This was no calm, serene hour of prayer. Matthew says that Jesus was "very sad and troubled" (26:37). The Master "fell to the ground" (26:39) and cried out to God. Luke tells us that Jesus was "full of pain" and that "his sweat was like drops of blood falling to the ground" (Luke 22:44).

Never has earth offered such an urgent request. And never has heaven offered more deafening silence. The prayer of Jesus was unanswered. *Jesus* and *unanswered prayer* in the same phrase? Isn't that an oxymoron? Would the son of Henry have no Ford or the child of Bill Gates own no computer? Would God, the one who owns the cattle on a thousand hills, keep something from his own son? He did that night. Consequently, Jesus had to deal with the dilemma of unanswered prayer. And that was just the beginning. Look who showed up next:

"With [Judas] were many people carrying swords and clubs who had been sent from the leading priests and the older Jewish leaders of the people. . . . Then the people came and grabbed Jesus and arrested him" (Matt. 26:47,51).

Judas arrived with an angry crowd. Again, from the perspective of an observer, this crowd represents another crisis. Not only did Jesus have to face unanswered prayer, he also had to deal with *unfruitful service*. The very people he came to save had now come to arrest him.

Let me give you a fact that may alter your impression of that night. Perhaps you envision Judas leading a dozen or so soldiers who are carrying two or three lanterns. Matthew tells us, however, that "many people" came to arrest Jesus. John is even more specific. The term he employs is the Greek word *speira* or a "group of soldiers" (John 18:3). At minimum, *speira* depicts a group of two hundred soldiers. It can describe a detachment as large as nineteen hundred![2]

Equipped with John's description, we'd be more accurate to imagine a river of several hundred troops entering the garden. Add to that figure untold watchers whom Matthew simply calls "the crowd," and you have a mob of people.

Surely in a group this size there is one person who will defend Jesus. He came to the aid of so many. All those sermons. All those miracles. Now they will bear fruit. And so we wait for the one person who will declare, "Jesus is an innocent man!" But no one does. Not one person speaks out on his behalf. The people he came to save have turned against him.

We can almost forgive the crowd. Their contact with Jesus

was too brief, too casual. Perhaps they didn't know better. But the disciples did. They knew better. They knew *him* better. But do they defend Jesus? Hardly. The most bitter pill Jesus had to swallow was the *unbelievable betrayal* by the disciples.

Judas wasn't the only turncoat. Matthew is admirably honest when he confesses, "All of Jesus' followers left him and ran away" (26:56).

For such a short word, *all* sure packs some pain. *"All* of Jesus' followers . . . ran away." John did. Matthew did. Simon did. Thomas did. They all did. We don't have to go far to find the last time this word was used. Note the verse just a few lines before our text: "But Peter said, 'I will never say that I don't know you! I will even die with you!' And *all* the other followers said the same thing" (26:35, italics mine).

All pledged loyalty, and yet *all* ran. From the outside looking in, all we see is betrayal. The disciples have left him. The people have rejected him. And God hasn't heard him. Never has so much trash been dumped on one being. Stack all the disloyalties of deadbeat dads and cheating wives and prodigal kids and dishonest workers in one pile, and you begin to see what Jesus had to face that night. From a human point of view, Jesus' world has collapsed. No answer from heaven, no help from the people, no loyalty from his friends.

Jesus, neck deep in rubbish. That's how I would have described the scene. That's how a reporter would have described it. That's how a witness would have portrayed it. But that's not how Jesus saw it. He saw something else entirely. He wasn't oblivious to the trash; he just wasn't limited to it. Somehow he was able to see good in the bad, the purpose in the pain, and God's presence in the problem.

We could use a little of Jesus' 20/20 vision, couldn't we? You and I live in a trashy world. Unwanted garbage comes our way on a regular basis. We, too, have unanswered prayers and unfruitful dreams and unbelievable betrayals, do we not? Haven't you been handed a trash sack of mishaps and heartaches? Sure you have. May I ask, what are you going to do with it?

SEEING WHAT JESUS SEES

You have several options. You could hide it. You could take the trash bag and cram it under your coat or stick it under your dress and pretend it isn't there. But you and I know you won't fool anyone. Besides, sooner or later it will start to stink. Or you could disguise it. Paint it green, put it on the front lawn, and tell everybody it is a tree. Again, no one will be fooled, and pretty soon it's going to reek. So what will you do? If you follow the example of Christ, you will learn to see tough times differently. Remember, God loves you just the way you are, but he refuses to leave you that way. He wants you to have a hope-filled heart . . . just like Jesus.

Here is what Christ did.

He found good in the bad. It would be hard to find someone worse than Judas. Some say he was a good man with a backfired strategy. I don't buy that. The Bible says, "Judas . . . was a thief. He was the one who kept the money box, and he often stole from it" (John 12:6). The man was a crook. Somehow he was able to live in the presence of God and experience the miracles of Christ and remain unchanged. In the end he decided he'd rather have money than a friend, so he sold Jesus for thirty pieces of silver. I'm sorry, but every human life is worth more than thirty pieces of silver. Judas was a scoundrel, a cheat, and a bum. How could anyone see him any other way?

I don't know, but Jesus did. Only inches from the face of his betrayer, Jesus looked at him and said, "Friend, do what you came to do" (Matt. 26:50). What Jesus saw in Judas as worthy of being called a friend, I can't imagine. But I do know that Jesus doesn't lie, and in that moment he saw something good in a very bad man.

It would help if we did the same. How can we? Again Jesus gives us guidance. He didn't place all the blame on Judas. He saw another presence that night: "this is . . . the time when darkness rules" (Luke 22:53). In no way was Judas innocent, but neither was Judas acting alone. Your attackers aren't acting alone either. "Our fight is not against people on earth but against the rulers and authorities and the powers of this world's darkness, against the spiritual powers of evil in the heavenly world" (Eph. 6:12).

Those who betray us are victims of a fallen world. We needn't place all the blame on them. Jesus found enough good in the face of Judas to call him friend, and he can help us do the same with those who hurt us.

Not only did Jesus find good in the bad, *he found purpose in the pain.* Of the ninety-eight words Jesus spoke at his arrest, thirty refer to the purpose of God.

"It must happen this way to bring about what the Scriptures say" (Matt. 26:54).

"All these things have happened so that it will come about as the prophets wrote" (v. 56).

Jesus chose to see his immediate struggle as a necessary part of a greater plan. He viewed the Gethsemane conflict as an important but singular act in the grand manuscript of God's drama.

I witnessed something similar on a recent trip. My daughter Andrea and I were flying to St. Louis. Because of storms, the flight was delayed and then diverted to another city where we sat on the runway waiting for the rain clouds to pass. As I was glancing at my watch and drumming my fingers, wondering when we would arrive, the fellow across the aisle tapped me on the arm and asked if he could borrow my Bible. I handed it to him. He turned to a young girl in the adjacent seat, opened the Bible, and the two read the Scriptures for the remainder of the trip.

After some time, the sky cleared, and we resumed our journey. We were landing in St. Louis when he returned the Bible to me and explained in a low voice that this was the girl's first flight. She'd recently joined the military and was leaving home for the first time. He asked her if she believed in Christ, and she said she wanted to but didn't know how. That's when he borrowed my Bible and told her about Jesus. By the time we landed, she told him she believed in Jesus as the Son of God.

I've since wondered about that event. Did God bring the storm so the girl could hear the gospel? Did God delay our arrival so she'd have ample time to learn about Jesus? I wouldn't put it past him. That is how Jesus chose to view the storm that came his way: necessary turbulence in the plan of God. Where others saw gray skies, Jesus saw a divine order. His suffering was necessary to fulfill prophecy, and his sacrifice was necessary to fulfill the law.

Wouldn't you love to have a hope-filled heart? Wouldn't you love to see the world through the eyes of Jesus? Where we see unanswered prayer, Jesus saw answered prayer. Where we see the absence of God, Jesus saw the plan of God. Note especially verse 53: "Surely you know I could ask my Father, and he would give me more than twelve armies of angels." Of all the treasures Jesus saw in the trash, this is most significant. He saw his father. He saw his father's presence in the problem. Twelve armies of angels were within his sight.

Sure, Max, but Jesus was God. He could see the unseen. He had eyes for heaven and a vision for the supernatural. I can't see the way he saw.

Not yet maybe, but don't underestimate God's power. He can change the way you look at life.

Need proof? How about the example of Elisha and his servant? The two were in Dothan when an angry king sent his army to destroy them.

> Elisha's servant got up early, and when he went out, he saw an army with horses and chariots all around the city. The servant said to Elisha, "Oh, my master, what can we do?"
>
> Elisha said, "Don't be afraid. The army that fights for us is larger than the one against us."

Then Elisha prayed, "LORD, open my servant's eyes, and let him see."

The LORD opened the eyes of the young man, and he saw that the mountain was full of horses and chariots of fire all around Elisha. (2 Kings 6:15–17)

By God's power, the servant saw the angels. Who is to say the same can't happen for you?

God never promises to remove us from our struggles. He does promise, however, to change the way we look at them. The apostle Paul dedicates a paragraph to listing trash bags: troubles, problems, sufferings, hunger, nakedness, danger, and violent death. These are the very Dumpsters of difficulty we hope to escape. Paul, however, states their value. "In all these things we have full victory through God" (Rom. 8:35–37). We'd prefer another preposition. We'd opt for *"apart* from all these things," or *"away* from all these things," or even, *"without* all these things." But Paul says, *"in"* all these things. The solution is not to avoid trouble but to change the way we see our troubles.

God can correct your vision.

He asks, "Who gives a person sight?" then answers, "It is I, the LORD" (Exod. 4:11). God let Balaam see the angel and Elisha see the army and Jacob see the ladder and Saul see the Savior. More than one have made the request of the blind man, "Teacher, I want to see" (Mark 10:51). And more than one have walked away with clear vision. Who is to say God won't do the same for you?

Sing to the LORD a new song;
sing to the LORD, all the earth.
Sing to the LORD and praise his name;
every day tell how he saves us.

PSALM 96:1–2

Rejoice that your names
are written in heaven.

LUKE 10:20 NIV

CHAPTER ELEVEN

WHEN HEAVEN CELEBRATES

A Rejoicing Heart

My family did something thoughtful for me last night. They had a party in my honor—a surprise birthday party. Early last week I told Denalyn not to plan anything except a nice, family evening at a restaurant. She listened only to the restaurant part. I was unaware that half a dozen families were going to join us.

In fact, I tried to talk her into staying at home. "Let's have the dinner on another night," I volunteered. Andrea had been sick. Jenna had homework, and I'd spent the afternoon watching football games and felt lazy. Not really in a mood to get up and clean up and go out. I thought I'd have no problem convincing the girls to postpone the dinner. Boy was I surprised! They wouldn't think of it. Each of my objections was met with a united front and a unanimous defense. My family made it clear—we were going out to eat.

Not only that, we were leaving on time. I consented and set about getting ready. But to their dismay, I moved too slowly. We were a study in contrasts. My attitude was *why hurry?* My daughters' attitude was *hurry up!* I was ho-hum. They were gung-ho. I was content to stay. They were anxious to leave. To be honest, I was bewildered by their actions. They were being uncharacteristically prompt. Curiously enthused. Why the big deal? I mean, I enjoy a night out as much as the next guy, but Sara giggled all the way to the restaurant.

Only when we arrived did their actions make sense. One step inside the door and I understood their enthusiasm. SURPRISE! No wonder they were acting differently. They knew what I didn't. They had seen what I hadn't. They'd already seen the table and stacked the gifts and smelled the cake. Since they knew about the party, they did everything necessary to see that I didn't miss it.

Jesus does the same for us. He knows about THE PARTY. In one of the greatest chapters in the Bible, Luke 15, he tells three stories. Each story speaks of something lost and of something found. A lost sheep. A lost coin. And a lost son. And at the end of each one, Jesus describes a party, a celebration. The shepherd throws the party for the lost-now-found sheep. The housewife throws a party because of the lost-now-found coin. And the father throws a party in honor of his lost-now-found son.

Three parables, each with a party. Three stories, each with the appearance of the same word: *happy*. Regarding the shepherd who found the lost sheep, Jesus says: "And when he finds it, he *happily* puts it on his shoulders and goes home" (vv. 5–6, italics mine). When the housewife finds her lost coin, she announces, "Be *happy* with me because I have found the coin that I lost" (v. 9, italics mine). And the father of the prodigal son explains to the reluctant older brother, "We had to celebrate and be *happy* because your brother was dead, but now he is alive. He was lost, but now he is found" (v. 32, italics mine).

The point is clear. Jesus is happiest when the lost are found. For him, no moment compares to the moment of salvation. For my daughter the rejoicing began when I got dressed and in the car and on the road to the party. The same occurs in heaven. Let one child consent to be dressed in righteousness and begin the journey home and heaven pours the punch, strings the streamers, and throws the confetti. "There is joy in the presence of the angels of God when one sinner changes his heart and life" (v. 10).

A century ago this verse caused Charles Spurgeon to write:

> There are Christmas days in heaven where Christ's high mass is kept, and Christ is not glorified because He was born in a manger but because he is born in a broken heart. And these are days when the shepherd brings home the lost sheep upon His shoulders, when the church has swept her house and found the lost piece of money, for then are these friends and neighbors called together, and they rejoice with joy unspeakable and full of glory over one sinner who repents.[1]

How do we explain such joy? Why such a stir? You've got to admit the excitement is a bit curious. We aren't talking about a nation of people or even a city of souls; we're talking about joy "when *one* sinner changes his heart and life." How could one person create that much excitement?

Who would imagine that our actions have such an impact on heaven? We can live and die and leave no more than an obituary. Our greatest actions on earth go largely unnoticed and unrecorded. Dare we think that God is paying attention?

According to this verse, he is. According to Jesus our decisions have a thermostatic impact on the unseen world. Our actions on the keyboard of earth trigger hammers on the piano strings of heaven. Our obedience pulls the ropes which ring the bells in heaven's belfries. Let a child call and the ear of the Father inclines. Let a sister weep and tears begin to flow from above. Let a saint die and the gate is opened. And, most important, let a sinner repent, and every other activity ceases, and every heavenly being celebrates.

Remarkable, this response to our conversion. Heaven throws no party over our other achievements. When we graduate from school or open our business or have a baby, as far as we know, the celestial bubbly stays in the refrigerator. Why the big deal over conversion?

We don't always share such enthusiasm, do we? When you hear of a soul saved, do you drop everything and celebrate? Is your good day made better or your bad day salvaged? We may be pleased—but exuberant? Do our chests burst with joy? Do we feel an urge to call out the band and cut the cake and have a party? When a soul is saved, the heart of Jesus becomes the night sky on the Fourth of July, radiant with explosions of cheer.

Can the same be said about us? Perhaps this is one area where our hearts could use some attention.

GOD'S MAGNUM OPUS

Why do Jesus and his angels rejoice over one repenting sinner? Can they see something we can't? Do they know something we don't? Absolutely. They know what heaven holds. They've seen the table, and they've heard the music, and they can't wait to see your face when you arrive. Better still, they can't wait to see you.

When you arrive and enter the party, something wonderful will happen. A final transformation will occur. You will be just like Jesus. Drink deeply from 1 John 3:2: "We have not yet been shown what we will be in the future. But we know that when Christ comes again, *we will be like him*" (italics mine).

Of all the blessings of heaven, one of the greatest will be you! You will be God's magnum opus, his work of art. The angels will gasp. God's work will be completed. At last, you will have a heart like his.

You will love with a perfect love.

You will worship with a radiant face.

You'll hear each word God speaks.

Your heart will be pure, your words will be like jewels, your thoughts will be like treasures.

You will be just like Jesus. You will, at long last, have a heart like his. Envision the heart of Jesus and you'll be envisioning your own. Guiltless. Fearless. Thrilled and joyous. Tirelessly worshiping. Flawlessly discerning. As the mountain stream is pristine and endless, so will be your heart. *You will be like him.*

And if that were not enough, everyone else will be like him as well. "Heaven is the perfect place for people made perfect."[2] Heaven is populated by those who let God change them. Arguments will cease, for jealousy won't exist. Suspicions won't surface, for there will be no secrets. Every sin is gone. Every insecurity is forgotten. Every fear is past. Pure wheat. No weeds. Pure gold. No alloy. Pure love. No lust. Pure hope. No fear. No wonder the angels rejoice when one sinner repents; they know another work of art will soon grace the gallery of God. They know what heaven holds.

There is yet another reason for the celebration. Part of the excitement is from our arrival. The other part is from our deliverance. Jesus rejoices that we are headed to heaven, but he equally rejoices that we are saved from hell.

WHAT WE'RE SAVED FROM

One phrase summarizes the horror of hell. "God isn't there."

Think for a moment about this question: What if God weren't here on earth? You think people can be cruel now, imagine us without the presence of God. You think we are brutal to each other now, imagine the world without the Holy Spirit. You think there is loneliness and despair and guilt now, imagine life without the touch of Jesus. No forgiveness. No hope. No acts of kindness. No words of love. No more food given in his name. No more songs sung to his praise. No more deeds done in his honor. If God took away his angels, his grace, his promise of eternity, and his servants, what would the world be like?

In a word, hell. No one to comfort you and no music to soothe you. A world where poets don't write of love and minstrels don't sing of hope, for love and hope were passengers on the last ship. The final vessel has departed, and the anthem of hell has only two words: "if only."

According to Jesus hell knows only one sound, the "weeping and gnashing of teeth" (Matt. 22:13 NIV). From hell comes a woeful, unending moan as its inhabitants realize the opportunity they have missed. What they would give for one more chance. But that chance is gone (Heb. 9:27).

POSSIBLE GODS AND GODDESSES

Can you see now why the angels rejoice when one sinner repents? Jesus knows what awaits the saved. He also knows what awaits the condemned. Can you see why we should rejoice as well? How can we? How can our hearts be changed so we rejoice like Jesus rejoices?

Ask God to help you have his eternal view of the world. His view of humanity is starkly simple. From his perspective every person is either:

- entering through the small gate or the wide gate (Matt. 7:13–14)

- traveling the narrow road or the wide road (Matt. 7:13–14)

- building on rock or sand (Matt. 7:24–27)

- wise or foolish (Matt. 25:2)

- prepared or unprepared (Matt. 24:45–51)

- fruitful or fruitless (Matt. 25:14–27)

- heaven called or hell bound (Mark 16:15–16)

At the sinking of the RMS *Titanic,* over twenty-two hundred people were cast into the frigid waters of the Atlantic. On shore the names of the passengers were posted in two simple columns—saved and lost.[3] God's list is equally simple.

Our ledger, however, is cluttered with unnecessary columns. Is he rich? Is she pretty? What work does he do? What color is her skin? Does she have a college degree? These matters are irrelevant to God. As he shapes us more and more to be like Jesus, they become irrelevant to us as well. "Our knowledge of men can no longer be based on their outward lives" (2 Cor. 5:16 PHILLIPS).

To have a heart like his is to look into the faces of the saved and rejoice! They are just one grave away from being just like Jesus. To have a heart like his is to look into the faces of the lost and pray. For unless they turn, they are one grave away from torment.

C. S. Lewis stated it this way:

It is a serious thing to live in a society of possible gods and goddesses, to remember that the dullest and most uninteresting person you talk to may one day be a creature which, if you saw it now, you would be strongly tempted to worship, or else a horror and a corruption such as now you meet only in a nightmare. All day long we are, in some degree, helping each other to one or the other of these destinations.[4]

And so my challenge to you is simple. Ask God to help you have his eternal view of the world. Every person you meet has been given an invitation to dinner. When one says yes, celebrate! And when one acts sluggish as I did last night, do what my daughters did. Stir him up and urge him to get ready. It's almost time for the party, and you don't want him to miss it.

Let us run the race that is
before us and never give up.

HEBREWS 12:1

CHAPTER TWELVE

FINISHING STRONG

An Enduring Heart

On one of my shelves is a book on power abs. The cover shows a closeup of a fellow flexing his flat belly. His gut has more ripples and ridges than a pond on a windy day. Inspired, I bought the book, read the routine, and did the sit-ups . . . for a week.

Not far from the power-abs book is a tape series on speed reading. This purchase was Denalyn's idea, but when I read the ad, I was equally enthused. The course promises to do for my mind what *Power Abs* promised to do for my gut—turn it into steel. The back-cover copy promises that mastering this six-week series will enable you to read twice as fast and retain twice the amount. All you have to do is listen to the tapes—which I intend to do . . . someday.

And then there is my bottle of essential minerals. Thirty-two ounces of pure health. One swallow a day and I'll ingest my quota of calcium, chloride, magnesium, sodium, and sixty-six other vital earthly elements. (There's even a trace of iron, which is good since I missed my shot at the iron abs and the steel-trap mind.) The enthusiast who sold me the minerals convinced me that thirty dollars was a small price to pay for good health. I agree. I just keep forgetting to take them.

Don't get me wrong. Not everything in my life is incomplete. (This book is finished . . . well, almost.) But I confess, I don't always finish what I start. Chances are I'm not alone. Any unfinished projects under your roof? Perhaps an exercise machine whose primary function thus far has been to hold towels? Or an unopened do-it-yourself pottery course? How about a half-finished patio deck or a half-dug pool or a half-planted garden? And let's not even touch the topic of diets and weight loss, OK?

You know as well as I, it's one thing to start something. It's something else entirely to complete it. You may think I'm going to talk to you about the importance of finishing everything. Could be you are bracing yourself for a bit of chastising.

If so, relax. "Don't start what you can't finish" is not one of my points. And I'm not going to say anything about what is used to pave the road to hell. To be honest, I don't believe you should finish everything you start. (Every student with homework just perked up.) There are certain quests better left undone, some projects wisely abandoned. (Though I wouldn't list homework as one of those.)

We can become so obsessed with completion that we become blind to effectiveness. Just because a project is on the table, doesn't mean it can't be returned to the shelf. No, my desire is not to convince you to finish everything. My desire is to encourage you to finish the *right* thing. Certain races are optional—like washboard abs and speed reading. Other races are essential—like the race of faith. Consider this admonition from the author of Hebrews: "Let us run the race that is before us and never give up" (Heb. 12:1).

THE RACE

Had golf existed in the New Testament era, I'm sure the writers would have spoken of mulligans and foot wedges, but it didn't, so they wrote about running. The word *race* is from the Greek *agon,* from which we get the word *agony.* The Christian's race is not a jog but rather a demanding and grueling, sometimes agonizing race. It takes a massive effort to finish strong.

Likely you've noticed that many don't? Surely you've observed there are many on the side of the trail? They used to be running. There was a time when they kept the pace. But then weariness set in. They didn't think the run would be this tough. Or they were discouraged by a bump and daunted by a fellow runner. Whatever the reason, they don't run anymore. They may be Christians. They may come to church. They may put a buck in the plate and warm a pew, but their hearts aren't in the race. They retired before their time. Unless something changes, their best work will have been their first work, and they will finish with a whimper.

By contrast, Jesus' best work was his final work, and his strongest step was his last step. Our Master is the classic example of one who endured. The writer of Hebrews goes on to say that Jesus "held on while wicked people were doing evil things to him" (v. 3). The Bible says Jesus "held on," implying that Jesus could have "let go." The runner could have given up, sat down, gone home. He could have quit the race. But he didn't. "He held on while wicked people were doing evil things to him."

THE RESISTANCE

Have you ever thought about the evil things done to Christ? Can you think of times when Jesus could have given up? How about his time of temptation? You and I know what it is like to endure a moment of temptation or an hour of temptation, even a day of temptation. But *forty* days? That is what Jesus faced. "The Spirit led Jesus into the desert where the devil tempted Jesus for forty days" (Luke 4:1–2).

We imagine the wilderness temptation as three isolated events scattered over a forty-day period. Would that it had been. In reality, Jesus' time of testing was nonstop; "the devil tempted Jesus for forty days." Satan got on Jesus like a shirt and refused to leave. Every step, whispering in his ear. Every turn of the path, sowing doubt. Was Jesus impacted by the devil? Apparently so. Luke doesn't say that Satan *tried* to tempt Jesus. The verse doesn't read, the devil *attempted* to tempt Jesus. No the passage is clear: "the devil *tempted* Jesus." Jesus was *tempted*, he was *tested*. Tempted to change sides? Tempted to go home? Tempted to settle for a kingdom on earth? I don't know, but I know he was tempted. A war raged within. Stress stormed without. And since he was tempted, he could have quit the race. But he didn't. He kept on running.

Temptation didn't stop him, nor did accusations. Can you imagine what it would be like to run in a race and be criticized by the bystanders?

Some years ago I entered a five-K race. Nothing serious, just a jog through the neighborhood to raise funds for a charity. Not being the wisest of runners, I started off at an impossible pace. Within a mile I was sucking air. At the right time, however, the spectators encouraged me. Sympathetic onlookers urged me on. One compassionate lady passed out cups of water, another sprayed us down with a hose. I had never seen these people, but that didn't matter. I needed a voice of encouragement, and they gave it. Bolstered by their assurance, I kept going.

What if in the toughest steps of the race, I had heard words of accusation and not encouragement? And what if the accusations came not from strangers I could dismiss but from my neighbors and family?

How would you like somebody to yell these words at you as you ran:

"Hey, liar! Why don't you do something honest with your life?" (see John 7:12).

"Here comes the foreigner. Why don't you go home where you belong?" (see John 8:48).

"Since when do they let children of the devil enter the race?" (see John 8:48).

That's what happened to Jesus. His own family called him a lunatic. His neighbors treated him even worse. When Jesus returned to his hometown, they tried to throw him off a cliff (Luke 4:29). But Jesus didn't quit running. Temptations didn't deter him. Accusations didn't defeat him. Nor did shame dishearten him.

I invite you to think carefully about the supreme test Jesus faced in the race. Hebrews 12:2 offers this intriguing statement: "[Jesus] accepted the shame as if it were nothing."

Shame is a feeling of disgrace, embarrassment, humiliation. Forgive me for stirring the memory, but don't you have a shameful moment in your history? Can you imagine the horror you would feel if everyone knew about it? What if a videotape of that event were played before your family and friends? How would you feel?

That is exactly what Jesus felt. *Why?* you ask. *He never did anything worthy of shame.* No, but we did. And since on the cross God made him become sin (2 Cor. 5:21), Jesus was covered with shame. He was shamed before his family. Stripped naked before his own mother and loved ones. Shamed before his fellow men. Forced to carry a cross until the weight caused him to stumble. Shamed before his church. The pastors and elders of his day mocked him, calling him names. Shamed before the city of Jerusalem. Condemned to die a criminal's death. Parents likely pointed to him from a distance and told their children, "That's what they do to evil men."

But the shame before men didn't compare with the shame Jesus felt before his father. Our individual shame seems too much to bear. Can you imagine bearing the collective shame of all humanity? One wave of shame after another was dumped on Jesus. Though he never cheated, he was convicted as a cheat. Though he never stole, heaven regarded him as a thief.

Though he never lied, he was considered a liar. Though he never lusted, he bore the shame of an adulterer. Though he always believed, he endured the disgrace of an infidel.

Such words stir one urgent question: How? How did he endure such disgrace? What gave Jesus the strength to endure the shame of all the world? We need an answer, don't we? Like Jesus we are tempted. Like Jesus we are accused. Like Jesus we are ashamed. But unlike Jesus, we give up. We give out. We sit down. How can we keep running as Jesus did? How can our hearts have the endurance Jesus had?

By focusing where Jesus focused: on "the joy that God put before him" (Heb. 12:2).

THE REWARD

This verse may very well be the greatest testimony ever written about the glory of heaven. Nothing is said about golden streets or angels' wings. No reference is made to music or feasts. Even the word *heaven* is missing from the verse. But though the word is missing, the power is not.

Remember, heaven was not foreign to Jesus. He is the only person to live on earth *after* he had lived in heaven. As believers, you and I will live in heaven after time on earth, but Jesus did just the opposite. He knew heaven before he came to earth. He knew what awaited him upon his return. And knowing what awaited him in heaven enabled him to bear the shame on earth.

He "accepted the shame as if it were nothing because of the

joy that God put before him" (Heb. 12:2). In his final moments, Jesus focused on the joy God put before him. He focused on the prize of heaven. By focusing on the prize, he was able not only to finish the race but to finish it strong.

I'm doing my best to do the same. In a far less significant ordeal, I, too, am seeking to finish strong. You are reading the next-to-last chapter of this book. For over a year I've lived with these pages: crafting thoughts, grooming paragraphs, pursuing the better verb, and digging for stronger conclusions. And now, the end is in sight.

Writing a book is much like running a long race. There is the initial burst of enthusiasm. Then the sags of energy. You give serious thought to giving up, but then a chapter will surprise you with a downhill slope. Occasionally an idea will inspire you. Often a chapter will tire you—not to mention those endless revisions demanded by relentless editors. But most of the work has the rhythm of a long-distance runner: long, sometimes lonely stretches at a steady pace.

And toward the end, with the finish line in sight and the editors content, there comes a numbing of the senses. You want to finish strong. You reach deep for the intensity you had months earlier, but the supply is scarce. The words blur, the illustrations run together, and the mind numbs. You need a kick, you need a surge, you need inspiration.

May I tell you where I find it? (This may sound peculiar, but bear with me.) Through years of writing at least one book a year, I've developed a ritual. Upon the completion of a project I enjoy a rite of celebration. I'm not into champagne, and I gave up cigars, but I have found something even sweeter. It involves two phases.

The first is a quiet moment before God. The moment the manuscript is in the mail, I find a secluded spot and stop. I don't say much, and, at least so far, neither does God. The purpose is not to talk as much as it is to relish. To delight in the sweet satisfaction of a completed task. Does a finer feeling exist? The runner feels the tape against his chest. It is finished. How sweet is the wine at the end of the journey. So for a few moments, God and I savor it together. We place the flag on the peak of Everest and enjoy the view.

Then (this really sounds mundane), I eat. I tend to skip meals during the homestretch, so I'm hungry. One year it was a Mexican dinner on the San Antonio River. Another it was room service and a basketball game. Last year I had catfish at a roadside café. Sometimes Denalyn joins me; other times I eat alone. The food may vary, and the company may change, but one rule remains constant. Throughout the meal I allow myself only one thought. *I am finished.* Planning future projects is not permitted. Consideration of tomorrow's tasks is not allowed. I indulge myself in a make-believe world and pretend that my life's work is complete.

And during that meal, in a minute way, I understand where Jesus found his strength. He lifted his eyes beyond the horizon and saw the table. He focused on the feast. And what he saw gave him strength to finish—and finish strong.

Such a moment awaits us. In a world oblivious to power abs and speed reading, we'll take our place at the table. In an hour that has no end, we will rest. Surrounded by saints and engulfed by Jesus himself, the work will, indeed, be finished. The final harvest will have been gathered, we will be seated, and Christ will christen the meal with these words: "Well done, good and faithful servant" (Matt. 25:23 KJV).

And in that moment, the race will have been worth it.

May he enlighten the eyes of your mind so that you can see what hope his call holds for you, what rich glories he has promised the saints will inherit.

EPHESIANS 1:18 NIV

❖⤳❖⤳❖

FIXING YOUR EYES ON JESUS

There are times when we see. And there are times when we *see.* Let me show you what I mean:

Everything changes the morning you see the "for sale" sign on your neighbor's boat. His deluxe bass boat. The bass boat you've coveted for three summers. All of a sudden nothing else matters. A gravitational tug pulls your car to the curb. You sigh as you behold your dream glistening in the sun. You run your fingers along the edge, pausing only to wipe the drool from your shirt. As you gaze, you are transported to Lake Tamapwantee, and it's just you and the glassy waters and your bass boat.

Or perhaps the following paragraph describes you better:

Everything changes the day you see him enter the English lit classroom. Just enough swagger to be cool. Just enough smarts to be classy. Not walking so fast as to be nervous, nor so slow as to be cocky. You've seen him before, but only in your dreams. Now he's really here. And you can't take your eyes off him. By the time class is over, you've memorized every curl and lash. And by the time this day is over, you resolve he's going to be yours.

There are times when we see. And then there are times when we *see*. There are times when we observe, and there are times when we memorize. There are times when we notice, and there are times when we study. Most of us know what it means to see a new boat or a new boy . . . but do we know what it's like to see Jesus? Do we know what it's like to "fix our eyes on Jesus" (Heb. 12:2 NIV)?

We've spent the last twelve chapters looking at what it means to be just like Jesus. The world has never known a heart so pure, a character so flawless. His spiritual hearing was so keen he never missed a heavenly whisper. His mercy so abundant he never missed a chance to forgive. No lie left his lips, no distraction marred his vision. He touched when others recoiled. He endured when others quit. Jesus is the ultimate model for every person. And what we have done in these pages is precisely what God invites you to do with the rest of your life. He urges you to fix your eyes upon Jesus. Heaven invites you to set the lens of your heart on the heart of the Savior and make him the object of your life. For that reason, I want us to close our time together with this question: What does it mean to *see* Jesus?

The shepherds can tell us. For them it wasn't enough to see the angels. You'd think it would have been. Night sky shattered with light. Stillness erupting with song. Simple shepherds roused from their sleep and raised to their feet by a choir of angels: "Glory to God in the highest!" Never had these men seen such splendor.

But it wasn't enough to see the angels. The shepherds wanted to see the one who sent the angels. Since they wouldn't be satisfied until they saw him, you can trace the long line of Jesus-seekers to a person of the pasture who said, "Let's go. . . . Let's *see*" (Luke 2:15, italics mine).

Not far behind the shepherds was a man named Simeon. Luke tells us Simeon was a good man who served in the temple during the time of Christ's birth. Luke also tells us, "Simeon had been told by the Holy Spirit that he would not die before he saw the Christ promised by the Lord" (Luke 2:26). This prophecy was fulfilled only a few days after the shepherds saw Jesus. Somehow Simeon knew that the blanketed bundle he saw in Mary's arms was the Almighty God. And for Simeon, seeing Jesus was enough. Now he was ready to die. Some don't want to die until they've seen the world. Simeon's dream was not so timid. He didn't want to die until he had seen the maker of the world. He had to see Jesus.

He prayed: "God, you can now release your servant; release me in peace as you promised. With *my own eyes* I've seen your salvation" (Luke 2:29–30 MSG, italics mine).

The Magi had the same desire. Like Simeon, they wanted to see Jesus. Like the shepherds, they were not satisfied with what they saw in the night sky. Not that the star wasn't spectacular. Not that the star wasn't historical. To be a witness of the blazing orb was a privilege, but for the Magi, it wasn't enough. It wasn't enough to see the light over Bethlehem; they had to see the Light of Bethlehem. It was him they came to see.

And they succeeded! They all succeeded. More remarkable than their diligence was Jesus' willingness. Jesus wanted to be seen! Whether they came from the pasture or the palace, whether they lived in the temple or among the sheep, whether their gift was of gold or honest surprise . . . they were welcomed. Search for one example of one person who desired to see the infant Jesus and was turned away. You won't find it.

You will find examples of those who didn't seek him. Those, like King Herod, who were content with less. Those, like the religious leaders, who preferred to read about him than to see him. The ratio between those who missed him and those who sought him is thousands to one. But the ratio between those who sought him and those who found him was one to one. *All who sought him found him.* Long before the words were written, this promise was proven: "God . . . rewards those who truly want to find him" (Heb. 11:6).

The examples continue. Consider John and Andrew. They, too, were rewarded. For them it wasn't enough to listen to John the Baptist. Most would have been content to serve in the shadow of the world's most famous evangelist. Could there be a better teacher? Only one. And when John and Andrew saw him, they left John the Baptist and followed Jesus. Note the request they made.

"Rabbi," they asked, "where are you staying?" (John 1:38). Pretty bold request. They didn't ask Jesus to give them a minute or an opinion or a message or a miracle. They asked for his address. They wanted to hang out with him. They wanted to know him. They wanted to know what caused his head to turn and his heart to burn and his soul to yearn. They wanted to study his eyes and follow his steps. They wanted to see him. They wanted to know what made him laugh and if he ever got tired. And most of all, they wanted to know, *Could Jesus be who John said he was—and if he is, what on earth is God doing on the earth?* You can't answer such a question by talking to his cousin; you've got to talk to the man himself.

Jesus' answer to the disciples? "Come and see" (v. 39). He didn't say, "Come and glance," or "Come and peek." He said, "Come and see." Bring your bifocals and binoculars. This is no time for side-glances or occasional peeks. "Let us fix our eyes on Jesus, the author and perfecter of our faith" (Heb. 12:2 NIV).

The fisherman fixes his eyes on the boat. The girl fixes her eyes on the boy. The disciple fixes his eyes on the Savior.

That's what Matthew did. Matthew, if you remember, was converted at work. According to his résumé, he was a revenue consultant for the government. According to his neighbors, he was a crook. He kept a tax booth and a hand extended at the street corner. That's where he was the day he saw Jesus. "Follow me," the Master said, and Matthew did. And in the very next verse we find Jesus sitting at Matthew's dining room table. "Jesus was having dinner at Matthew's house" (Matt. 9:10).

A curbside conversion couldn't satisfy his heart, so Matthew took Jesus home. Something happens over a dinner table that doesn't happen over an office desk. Take off the tie, heat up the grill, break out the sodas, and spend the evening with the suspender of the stars. "You know, Jesus, forgive me for asking but I've always wanted to know . . ."

Again, though the giving of the invitation is impressive, the acceptance is more so. Didn't matter to Jesus that Matthew was a thief. Didn't matter to Jesus that Matthew had built a split-level house with the proceeds of extortion. What did matter was that Matthew wanted to know Jesus, and since God "rewards those who truly want to find him" (Heb. 11:6), Matthew was rewarded with the presence of Christ in his home.

Of course, it only made sense that Jesus spend time with Matthew. After all, Matthew was a top draft pick, shoulder-tapped to write the first book of the New Testament. Jesus hangs out with only the big guys like Matthew and Andrew and John. Right?

May I counter that opinion with an example? Zacchaeus was far from a big guy. He was small, so small he couldn't see over the crowd that lined the street the day Jesus came to Jericho. Of course the crowd might have let him elbow up to the front, except that he, like Matthew, was a tax collector. But he, like Matthew, had a hunger in his heart to see Jesus.

It wasn't enough to stand at the back of the crowd. It wasn't enough to peer through a cardboard telescope. It wasn't enough to listen to someone else describe the parade of the Messiah. Zacchaeus wanted to see Jesus with his own eyes.

So he went out on a limb. Clad in a three-piece Armani suit and brand-new Italian loafers, he shimmied up a tree in hopes of seeing Christ.

I wonder if you would be willing to do the same. Would you go out on a limb to see Jesus? Not everyone would. In the same Bible where we read about Zacchaeus crawling across the limb, we read about a young ruler. Unlike Zacchaeus, the crowd parted to make room for him. He was the . . . ahem . . . *rich, young ruler.* Upon learning that Jesus was in the area, he called for the limo and cruised across town and approached the carpenter. Please note the question he had for Jesus: "Teacher, what good thing must I do to have life forever?" (Matt. 19:16).

Bottom line sort of fellow, this ruler. No time for formalities or conversations. "Let's get right to the issue. Your schedule is busy; so is mine. Tell me how I can get saved, and I'll leave you alone."

There was nothing wrong with his question, but there was a problem with his heart. Contrast his desire with that of Zacchaeus, "Can I make it up that tree?"

Or John and Andrew, "Where are you staying?"
Or Matthew, "Can you spend the evening?"
Or Simeon, "Can I stay alive until I see him?"
Or the Magi, "Saddle up the camels. We aren't stopping until we find him."
Or the shepherd, "Let's go. . . . Let's see."

See the difference? The rich, young ruler wanted medicine. The others wanted the Physician. The ruler wanted an answer to the quiz. They wanted the teacher. He was in a hurry. They had all the time in the world. He settled for a cup of coffee at the drive-through window. They wouldn't settle for anything less than a full-course meal at the banquet table. They wanted more than salvation. They wanted the Savior. They wanted to see Jesus.

They were earnest in their search. One translation renders Hebrews 11:6: "God . . . rewards those who *earnestly* seek him" (NIV, italics mine).

Another reads: "God rewards those who *search* for him" (PHILLIPS, italics mine).

And another: "God . . . rewards those who *sincerely look* for him" (TLB, italics mine).

I like the King James translation: "He is a rewarder of them that *diligently* seek him" (italics mine).

Diligently—what a great word. Be diligent in your search. Be hungry in your quest, relentless in your pilgrimage. Let this book be but one of dozens you read about Jesus and this hour be but one of hundreds in which you seek him. Step away from the puny pursuits of possessions and positions, and seek your king.

Don't be satisfied with angels. Don't be content with stars in the sky. Seek him out as the shepherds did. Long for him as Simeon did. Worship him as the wise men did. Do as John and Andrew did: ask for his address. Do as Matthew: invite Jesus into your house. Imitate Zacchaeus. Risk whatever it takes to see Christ.

God rewards those who seek *him*. Not those who seek doctrine or religion or systems or creeds. Many settle for these lesser passions, but the reward goes to those who settle for nothing less than Jesus himself. And what is the reward? What awaits those who seek Jesus? Nothing short of the heart of Jesus. "And as the Spirit of the Lord works within us, we become more and more like him" (2 Cor. 3:18 TLB).

Can you think of a greater gift than to be like Jesus? Christ felt no guilt; God wants to banish yours. Jesus had no bad habits; God wants to remove yours. Jesus had no fear of death; God wants you to be fearless. Jesus had kindness for the diseased and mercy for the rebellious and courage for the challenges. God wants you to have the same.

He loves you just the way you are, but he refuses to leave you that way. He wants you to be just like Jesus.

NOTES

CHAPTER 1: A HEART LIKE HIS

1. Adapted from Max Lucado, *A Gentle Thunder* (Dallas: Word Publishing, 1995), 46.

2. David Jeremiah audiotape: *The God of the Impossible,* TPR02.

CHAPTER 2: LOVING THE PEOPLE YOU ARE STUCK WITH

1. Max Lucado, Ph.D. of Etymological Contortionism, *Max's Manual of Medical Terms* (Nonsense, Tex.: One Page Publishing, 1998), vol. 1, ch. 1, p. 1, sentence 1.

CHAPTER 3: THE TOUCH OF GOD

1. Not his actual name.

CHAPTER 4: HEARING GOD'S MUSIC

1. Matt. 11:15, 13:9, 13:43; Mark 4:9, 4:23, 8:18; Luke 8:8, 14:35; Rev. 2:7, 2:11, 2:17, 2:29, 3:6, 3:13, 3:22, 13:9.

2. Mark 4:1–20.

3. Rev. 2:7, 2:11, 2:17, 2:29, 3:6, 3:13, 3:22.

CHAPTER 5:

BEING LED BY AN UNSEEN HAND

1. Brother Lawrence and Frank Laubach, *Practicing His Presence,* (Goleta, CA: Christian Books, 1973.) Used by kind permission of Dr. Robert S. Laubach and Gene Edwards.

2. Ibid.

3. Ibid.

4. Ibid.

5. As quoted in Timothy Jones, *The Art of Prayer* (New York: Ballantine Books, 1997), 133.

6. Ibid., 140.

7. Charles R. Swindoll, *The Finishing Touch* (Dallas: Word Publishing, 1994), 292.

CHAPTER 6:

A CHANGED FACE AND A SET OF WINGS

1. Matt. 7:7 NIV.

2. Horatio G. Spafford, "It Is Well with My Soul."

CHAPTER 7:

GOLF GAMES AND CELERY STICKS

1. John Maxwell, *Developing the Leader within You* (Nashville: Thomas Nelson, 1993), 29.

CHAPTER 8: NOTHING BUT THE TRUTH

1. James Hassett, "But That Would Be Wrong," *Psychology Today,* November 1981, 34–41.

2. Paul Lee Tan, *Encyclopedia of 7700 Illustrations* (Rockville, Md.: Assurance Publishers, 1979), 562–63.

CHAPTER 10: FINDING GOLD IN THE GARBAGE

1. Jim Morrison, "Slightly Rotted Gold," *American Way Magazine,* 1 April 1992, 32–35.

2. William Barclay, *The Gospel of John,* vol. 2 (Philadelphia: The Westminster Press, 1975), 222.

CHAPTER 11: WHEN HEAVEN CELEBRATES

1. Charles Spurgeon's sermon entitled "The Sympathy of Two Worlds," quoted in John MacArthur, *The Glory of Heaven* (Wheaton, IL: Crossway Books, 1996), 246.

2. Ibid., 118.

3. James Ryle, unpublished manuscript. Used by permission.

4. C. S. Lewis, *The Weight of Glory* (New York: Macmillan, 1949), 14–15.

STUDY GUIDE

ONE

A HEART LIKE HIS

Finding the Heart of Jesus

1. What would change in your life if Jesus really did become you?

    A. Who would be surprised at the "new you"? Why?

    B. Would you have "fences to mend"? If so, to whom do they belong?

2. Since God wants you to have a heart like his ("a new person, made to be like God," says Ephesians 4:23–24), give yourself a checkup:

    A. What's your heart condition today?

    B. What would happen during a spiritual "stress test"? Would the results differ, depending on what was happening in your life from day to day? Explain.

    C. What specific actions would you have to take to develop a heart like Jesus'?

3. God wants you to be like him, but he does love you just the way you are. Describe the "you" that God loves.

A. What are your gifts, talents, abilities, concerns, cares, quirks, faults, needs, desires?

B. How would any of those be different if you had "a heart like his"? Which parts of you would be "tweaked"?

4. Jesus' thoughts, actions, and entire self reflected his intimate relationship with his father. As a result, his heart was supremely spiritual.

A. Describe a "spiritual heart."

B. Describe any differences between your heart and that of Christ.

5. As Max points out, we've "tapped into" God's power, but not enough of us use it to its full extent.

A. Describe your "power usage." How much of his light do you use at work? At home? In your community?

B. What can you learn from reflecting on the heart of Christ?

Probing the Mind of Jesus

1. Read Philippians 2:5–13.

A. We are to have the same attitude as Christ, to "think and act like Christ Jesus." How difficult is this for you? What is difficult about it? Explain.

B. How much effort are you willing to expend to comply with the directive of this passage? What kind of effort?

C. What about your heart needs the most attention?

2. Ephesians 4:20–32 deals with some specific no-no's for those Christians who want to live as "children of light."

   A. Which part of your "old self" gives you the most trouble?

   B. What can you determine today to do about this?

3. Jesus was sinless—his words and actions were always pure. Read 1 John 3:1–10.

   A. How does it make you feel to know you have an example like this? Is it intimidating or comforting to you? Explain.

   B. Jesus has given his sinless self to you and is waiting to remake you into someone just like himself. How can you use this thought to motivate you to become like him? Does it? Explain.

Becoming the Hands of Jesus

1. Write down Colossians 3:10 on a card and post it where you will see it every day. Memorize it and thank God for loving you enough to change you into someone like him!

2. Spend a few minutes imagining yourself handling a particular prickly situation, one that you usually struggle with. Now imagine how you could handle it with "a heart like his." Then pray that God will enable you to handle an actual situation just as you did in your imagination. The next time it occurs, write in a journal what happened, and see how God will answer your honest prayers!

TWO

LOVING THE PEOPLE
YOU ARE STUCK WITH

A Forgiving Heart

Finding the Heart of Jesus

1. Consider "the claustrophobia that comes with commitment."

    A. Have you experienced commitment claustrophobia?

    B. Where do you encounter this—with a spouse, child, employee, or someone else? Explain.

    C. Have you ever felt fearful or frustrated because of the permanence involved in commitment? If so, describe your reaction.

    D. If you feel "stuck" with someone right now (with a major case of stuckititus), do you feel most like fleeing, fighting, or forgiving? Explain.

    E. How would you feel if you knew that person felt the same way about you? Do you think anyone does? If so, explain.

2. Jesus was able to love people who were even hard to like.

    A. Name some folks you find hard to like. Why is this?

    B. Name some folks who may find you hard to like. Why is this?

3. Jesus knew no one "expected" him to do the work of the lowliest servant when he washed the feet of the disciples as described in John 13. Remember he was fully aware that they would desert him in his greatest hour of need—yet he served them with a heart bursting with love.

   A. If footwashing were still a custom today, would you be willing to serve one of the people you named in study question 1 or 2 above in such a way? Explain.

   B. Think of someone who "washed your feet" when you didn't deserve it. What were the circumstances?

4. As you shift your gaze away from your "problem person" and onto Jesus, what happens to your ability to forgive that person?

   A. Name the sins for which Christ has had to forgive you this day alone. Are any of them "repeats"? Explain.

   B. Realizing all the clean-up duty Jesus has had to perform on you, how willing are you to do the same for others? How do you respond to those who continually, repeatedly, cause you the same problems?

5. Max reminds us there was only one man in that Passover Supper room worthy of having his feet washed, and that was the footwasher himself. The one who should have been served chose to become the servant.

   A. Name several relationships you could improve by doing some unexpected footwashing.

B. How could you "wash" someone's "feet"? How do you think it would be received? Explain.

C. Do any of the people involved sit at your supper table? If so, is this kind of footwashing easier or harder? Why?

Probing the Mind of Jesus

1. Meditate on Colossians 3:12–17.

    A. Insert people's names where appropriate in this passage ("Bear with _____, and forgive whatever grievances you may have against _____.")

    B. Now repeat this exercise, asking God to help someone bear with you.

2. Put yourself into the scene described in John 13:1–17.

    A. You're sitting there, waiting. And waiting. Just where is that wretched servant anyway? Then your Master, of all people, gets up to do the work. How do you feel, watching while he is working? What are you thinking?

    B. If you were at this scene and knew what Judas was about to do, would you have washed his feet as Jesus did? Explain.

3. Ephesians 4:32 says, "Be kind and loving [or compassionate] to each other, and forgive each other just as God forgave you in Christ." Read the next verse (Eph. 5:1).

A. How grimy did God get when he reached down to clean you up? How grimy are you willing to get in order to be an "imitator of God"?

B. Ephesians 5:2 continues, "And live a life of love, just as Christ loved us and gave himself up for us as a fragrant offering and sacrifice to God." With God's help, what kind of changes do you need to make in order to make your life a sweet-smelling sacrifice? Explain.

C. Is there a Judas in your life? Can you do for him what Jesus did for his Judas?

Becoming the Hands of Jesus

1. Thank God for his daily mercy and forgiveness. Express your gratitude for his limitless grace. Meditate on the biblical truth that he remembers your sins no more, but they are as far from him as "the east is from the west"!

2. The wronged wife in the story at the end of this chapter was merciful to her husband. She forgave and was willing to let go of her hurt. She said, "Let's move on." Think of a person who has wounded you. Determine today that you will start this same process. Ask God to help you bathe his/her feet in his love, and deliberately forget the hurt. Spend time in prayer about this person and the situation. Ask God to help you know how to forgive the hurt and love the person just as Jesus does.

THREE

THE TOUCH OF GOD
A Compassionate Heart

Finding the Heart of Jesus

1. Remember some instances when "God's very hands" ministered to you. How did this make you feel?

2. Do you think you have the "hands of heaven"? Explain. Do you make it a practice to seek out opportunities to care for others with those hands?

3. Have you ever "quarantined" someone from your life?

   A. If so, what was/is the situation? Why did you make the exclusion?

   B. What would cause you to include him/her once again?

4. Though Jesus' words cured the leper's disease, Max points out that only Christ's loving touch banished the man's loneliness.

   A. Describe some periods in your life when no words came, but a touch said it all.

   B. Is talking about "godly touching" easier than actually doing it? Explain.

   C. Do you find it easy or difficult to receive such a touch? Why?

5. Make a list of ways to "touch" someone emotionally without physically touching them (Here's a start: cards, visits, etc.)

Probing the Mind of Jesus

1. Read again the story of the cleansed leper from Matthew 8:1–4. Read also Mark 1:40–45 and Luke 5:12–16. All three writers mention the touch of Jesus, as well as his healing words.

   A. Why do you think Jesus thought it was important to physically touch the man?

   B. Would the story have been diminished without the touch? Explain.

2. The Mark account states that the cleansed leper, though having been warned not to tell the story to anyone, instead went out and began to talk freely.

   A. Why did Jesus command the man to be silent?

   B. What happened when the man spoke out?

   C. Would you have been able to keep quiet if such a marvelous thing had happened to you? Explain.

3. The niv rendering of Colossians 3:12 states that we are to "clothe [ourselves] with compassion and kindness." Dressing is a deliberate act; we intentionally do it and it never "just happens." But as we do it every day, it becomes a natural act.

A. Think of someone who has a compassionate spirit? How is this spirit expressed through his/her actions, speech, demeanor?

B. With the Lord's help, how can you work at better showing compassion?

Becoming the Hands of Jesus

1. Spend a few minutes thanking the Lord for those who have taken the time to show you compassion or kindness when you needed it most. Bring them by name before the Lord. Then tell them personally, through a note or phone call, what their ministry to you has meant.

2. Ask God to show you someone who needs that special "godly touch." Chances are you already know who it is. If you sense some resistance on your part ("Not him/her! Not me—I can't!"), ask the Lord to make your hands into his and surrender them to him. Then follow as he leads you.

FOUR

✦✦✦✦

HEARING GOD'S MUSIC
A Listening Heart

Finding the Heart of Jesus

1. Scripture often reminds us that it's not enough to have ears—we must use them. The problem is, we often don't.

A. We are to "listen like sheep" who follow their master's well-known voice. How do you try to hear God's voice on a regular basis?

B. How can you become so familiar with the Master that you'd know "a stranger's voice" immediately? How can you recognize false teaching when you hear it?

2. Jesus made it a habit to pray. Max says Christ "cleared his calendar" in order to speak with his father.

A. Describe your own prayer life. Do days ever go by when you realize you've totally neglected this privilege? How did those days go for you?

B. What would happen to your marriage/family/friendship/work relationships if your communication with the people in them was the same as that between you and your Savior?

3. Jesus was intimately familiar with Scripture.

A. Christ knew the Bible and how to use it. How's your scripture memory?

B. How easy is it for you to locate a specific verse?

C. Do you understand most Scripture well enough to apply it effectively? Explain.

D. How are you at explaining Scripture to others, especially those who don't yet know Christ?

4. If we want to be like Jesus, we need to let God have us.

A. Do you really want to be "had"? Explain.

B. How can you surrender your entire life, your whole being, to him? Be specific.

C. When is the best time for you to spend the necessary time listening for him in Bible study and prayer, until you have received your lesson for each day? Do you take advantage of this time?

5. The Bible says we are worthy because of what Christ did for us; we did nothing to deserve such a lofty status. Because of this, he wants us to open our hearts completely to him.

A. How do you react to such undeserved affection? Why?

B. What happens between you and God when you open your heart to him?

Probing the Mind of Jesus

1. Read the parable of the sower in Mark 4:1–20.

A. Give yourself a checkup: Which seed describes you best? Why?

B. What kind of changes might be needed to make you into seed sown on good soil, producing a crop a hundred times over?

2. John 10:1–18 describes the relationship between a shepherd and his sheep, as well as that between the Lord and his people. The passage says sheep will "run away" from strangers

because they do not recognize them. They are so attuned to their master that they want no other, and the master is so in love with his sheep he will die for them.

A. What benefits do sheep receive by sticking close to their master?

B. What dangers lurk if they choose to wander away?

C. Do you think sheep fret over their "worthiness"? Explain.

D. What parallels can you draw between sheep and people?

3. If we want to be like Jesus, we must have a regular time of talking to God and listening to his Word.

A. Romans 12 contains a list of "do's" for those who wish to live in harmony with the Lord and with others. Why are we to do these things? How are we to do them?

B. How can you make your prayer times worshipful?

C. Define "being faithful in prayer."

D. Is it possible to be faithful in prayer without spending time in the Word? Explain.

Becoming the Hands of Jesus

1. Living in the communications age, we are inundated with so much information that we can become overloaded. News-papers, magazines, television, and the Internet all scream for our attention. Challenge yourself this week to spend as many or more hours reading the Bible as you do with your paper or TV. Then record the difference it makes in your life.

2. If you don't already do so, keep a journal of your journey with the Lord. For one month, record the passages you study and the amount of time you spend with him in prayer as a result. Track the positive changes you find in your relationship with the Lord as well as with others.

FIVE

❧✦✧

BEING LED BY AN UNSEEN HAND
A God-Intoxicated Heart

Finding the Heart of Jesus

1. We are always in the presence of God.

   A. Does the statement above comfort you or tire you? Why?

   B. What does the reality of God's continuous presence mean to you as you go about your everyday activities?

2. God wants us to enjoy the same intimacy with him that he has with his Son.

   A. Do you like intimacy or do you prefer standing a bit apart, keeping your "space"? Explain.

   B. How do you try to keep parts of yourself hidden from others? What would you like to keep hidden from God?

3. God is never away from us.

   A. Have you ever found yourself feeling especially close to God on Sunday morning but miles away by Tuesday afternoon? If so, describe this experience. Why do you think this happens?

   B. God is absolutely committed to us and provides a model for us. What is your level of commitment—to your spouse, your children, your church, etc.? Are they secure in the knowledge you'll never leave and you'll always be there for them? How have you conveyed to them your commitment?

4. In the Christian's "marriage to Jesus," the communication never stops.

   A. When you talk to God, what do you mention first? Does the giving of praise and honor regularly come before the litany of requests? If not, why not?

   B. How long would a friendship last if the only communication between two people was the asking of favors? Would you long for something else, for something deeper? Explain.

   C. Is God the first person to whom you talk when something great happens to you? Is he the last when you have a problem? Explain.

5. Consider every moment in your life a potential time of communion with God.

A. Do you know anyone else besides God who would really want to hear from you all the time?

B. How is your sense of worth affected by knowing God will never leave you? Does this change your worship of him?

Probing the Mind of Jesus

1. First Corinthians 6:1 names believers as God's "fellow workers," or to put it more commonly, God's "coworkers."

   A. What would happen to your everyday work ethic if you truly believed yourself to be working right alongside the one true God? Would you work harder? Would you do your best at everything with God at the next workstation? Explain.

   B. Should life itself be easier to handle, knowing the Almighty is going through it right along with you? If so, how?

2. Read John 5:16–30.

   A. Jesus said the Son did "nothing by himself"; what the Father did, the Son did. Can the same be said of you? Why? What causes you to run ahead of God? What areas of your life do you try to handle without God's help?

   B. Jesus also didn't attempt to please himself but his father (v. 30). Who are you most trying to please? Your spouse? Your parents? The neighbors?

3. God's word picture of a vine and its branches in John 15:1–8 describes the relationship he desires with his people. He wants to be completely connected to us.

   A. How does your desire for intimacy with God compare to that of Frank Laubach, who felt lost after just a half-hour without thinking of him?

   B. List some practical ways your life would change if you were this connected.

   C. Jesus talks of pruning the branches that bear fruit so they will become even more fruitful. Describe a time you felt the effects of his pruning knife. What kind of fruit was borne afterward? Do you desire even bigger, better fruit, even if you must be pruned again and again? Explain.

Becoming the Hands of Jesus

1. Ask the Lord for two special verses: one to meditate on when you awake and one for the evening as you retire. Do it faithfully for at least a solid week. Use those bookends to begin directing your whole day toward a totally God-centered life.

2. God already knows what you're thinking, wanting, and doing. Realize that he wants to hear from you, so begin talking to him as if he were on the car seat beside you in the morning, standing in the line at the bank, or sitting at

the next desk. He's not interested in flowery phrases or pious sounding words—he just wants you.

SIX

❧❀❧

A CHANGED FACE AND A SET OF WINGS
A Worship-Hungry Heart

Finding the Heart of Jesus

1. Describe a time you met a famous person or attended a very important event. Did you buy a new dress or suit? Were you thinking about it for days beforehand? How important was the famous person or the event compared to a meeting with Jesus?

2. How do you define worship? What is involved?

   A. Why do you worship?

   B. Is worship more or less important to you today than when you first came to know the Lord?

3. Jesus prepared himself for worship, yet we're often casual when it comes to meeting God.

   A. Think about a typical Sunday morning before you leave for church. Be honest with yourself. Do tempers flare? Are you rushing around? Describe the day.

B. What could you do to improve the situation, even beginning the night before? What keeps you from implementing these changes?

4. God changes our faces through worship.

   A. How can you give more conscious thought to the words you're singing, praying, or hearing?

   B. What happens to your face as you leave the service and head to your work week?

   C. Would anyone know by looking at you on Tuesday that you'd been with the Master on Sunday? How?

5. God changes those who watch us worship.

   A. What aspects of your worship are designed to attract people who don't know Christ?

   B. How often during the service do you take time to pray for any unsaved people who might be sitting alongside you?

Probing the Mind of Jesus

1. Read Matthew 17:1–9.

   A. Do you think the disciples understood the purpose of their worship trip to the mountain?

   B. How do you think they were affected by their experience? (Read 1 Peter 1:16–18.)

C. Why do you suppose Christ told them to tell no one about it?

2. Second Corinthians 3:12–18 contrasts Moses' wearing a veil to mask God's glory with the believer's privilege of an unveiled face.

   A. How do we sometimes present "veiled faces" or hearts as we worship? Why do we do this?

   B. How can you best "reflect God's glory" this week? At home? At work? With friends?

3. Read Psalm 34 silently to yourself, then read it aloud.

   A. How "big" does God seem to you in this passage? What words would you use to describe God and his glory?

   B. Read through the passage again and count the number of reasons there are to praise God.

   C. Now look at your face in a mirror. Do you see God's reflection? Explain.

Becoming the Hands of Jesus

1. If Sunday mornings before church are a problem at your house, sit down with your family and talk it through. See if anyone else has been concerned. Determine to make physical, practical preparations the night before (find that lost shoe, make clothing decisions, etc.). Take time for a meeting with the Lord at home before you meet him at

church. And remember: he is reachable in the car on the way, too!

2. Whether you're the "official greeter" at your church or not, consider making this your mission opportunity next Sunday. Instead of waiting for visitors to make themselves known, put God's smile on your face, and purposefully seek them out.

SEVEN

❧❦❧

GOLF GAMES AND CELERY STICKS
A Focused Heart

Finding the Heart of Jesus

1. One of the incredible traits of Jesus was his ability to stay on target.

   A. How on track is your life? Explain.

   B. Where do you want to go in your life? Name some specific goals you have.

2. Our lives tend to be scattered.

   A. In what way(s) does this statement reflect your life?

   B. What are your priorities?

   C. Are you easily distracted by the small things and forgetful about the big things? Explain.

3. God wants us to have focused hearts, to stay on target, to fit into God's plan.

   A. What is God's plan concerning you?

   B. How do your plans compare with those of God? Explain.

4. When we submit to God's plans, we can trust our desires.

   A. If whatever you desired came to be, do you think it would be good for you? Explain.

   B. How can you commit yourself to whatever God wants for you, even if it might be different from what you desire?

5. In Romans 12:3 Paul advises that we should "have a sane estimate of [our] capabilities."

   A. You are probably aware of your weaknesses, but what are your strengths?

   B. How are you using those strengths to serve and honor God? Have you thanked him for them?

Probing the Mind of Jesus

1. Read Mark 10:42–45.

   A. What kind of ruler was Jesus describing in verse 42?

   B. How should the behavior of "those who want to be great" differ from the actions of others?

   C. How do you think things would have changed if Jesus had chosen to "be served" instead of to serve?

2. Compare Mark 10:45 with Luke 19:10.

    A. Do these two verses say the same thing? Why or why not?

    B. Would you consider one or both to be Christ's "mission statement"? Explain.

3. Romans 8:28 has often been quoted and misquoted.

    A. How does this verse function when so-called "bad things" happen to us?

    B. Do you think God "plans" the "bad things" or that he just allows them? Is it the same thing?

    C. Continue reading from verse 28 to the end of the chapter. Describe how these verses relate to the "bad things" in your life.

4. God wants to use us to bring about his plan. (Read 2 Corinthians 5:17–21).

    A. What are you doing to serve as Christ's representative or ambassador?

    B. What tools do you have to prepare you for this work? How are you using them?

5. Spend some time in Psalm 37.

    A. How much time do you spend fretting over "evil men"? Are you ever worried they won't "get theirs"? Explain.

    B. What does God say will happen to them?

    C. What should you be doing instead of worrying about retribution?

D. When your heart and God's come together, what happens to your desires?

Becoming the Hands of Jesus

1. Both Psalm 139:14 and Ephesians 2:10 declare God's marvelous workmanship in you. Do you believe them? Take a few moments to write down the specific things about you that illustrate that statement. Dedicate those qualities to the Lord and determine to start using them for him today.

2. When you were little did anyone ask, "What do you want to be when you grow up?" How did your answer then compare with today? As you've grown up in the Lord, what do you want to be, to do, for him? Spend some time in prayer and then compose a personal life mission statement, with which you can serve and honor God.

EIGHT

NOTHING BUT THE TRUTH
An Honest Heart

Finding the Heart of Jesus

1. The Christian is a witness.

A. What's the difference between a witness in court and a witness for Christ?

B. We know there's a penalty for perjury in court. Is there one for the Christian? Explain.

2. Jesus didn't lie, cheat, or stretch the truth.

   A. How do you measure up to God's standard in this area?

   B. Do you think there's a difference between "regular" lies and "white" ones? Explain.

   C. Once you realize you've been dishonest, what do you do about it? Does it depend on how big the lie was? Explain.

3. God is as angry about lying as he is about such things as adultery and aggravated assault.

   A. Do you agree with this viewpoint? Explain.

   B. How can you strive to live out God's honor code? What do you do when you fall short?

4. God always speaks the truth. The Bible says he "cannot lie."

   A. In what circumstances are you most tempted to lie?

   B. Do others consider you to be an honest person? Would your assessment and theirs differ?

   C. How do you feel about lying or evading the truth a little in order to spare the feelings of others?

5. There are times when the truth is difficult.

   A. Name some situations in which we are more comfortable with a lie than the truth.

B. How is it possible to lie without using words?

C. We know there are consequences to lying. Have you ever been caught in a lie? What happened? How did you feel? What did you learn from these consequences?

Probing the Mind of Jesus

1. Read Ephesians 4:17–32. Paul admonishes his readers to get rid of their former way of life and display a "new attitude of the mind."

   A. Since Christians are members of one body, is it worse to be dishonest with a fellow believer than with one who is not? Explain.

   B. How can you be dishonest with yourself?

   C. Do you agree that lying should be placed in the same category with anger, theft, foul language, etc.? Do you "rank" sins, considering some worse than others? Explain.

2. Spend some time in Psalm 101.

   A. What do you do when others are "slandering [their] neighbor in secret"?

   B. What kind of company do you keep? Do you tolerate liars?

3. Titus 1:2 and 2 Timothy 2:13 remind us that we can always believe God.

A. How should this truth affect our everyday lives? Does it? Explain.

B. Which of God's promises are most precious to you? Why?

C. When you promise something, can you be relied upon? Explain.

4. Think about the story of Ananias and Sapphira in Acts 5.

A. Why do you think this couple lied about the price of the land? Why didn't they tell Peter they were just giving a portion of what they received?

B. Do you think Ananias and Sapphira ever thought they would be found out? Why or why not?

C. What was it about this lie that angered Peter?

D. How do you feel about the harsh punishment God meted out? How would their witness for Christ in the community have been affected had they not been so judged? What happened to the witness of the church after their deaths?

Becoming the Hands of Jesus

1. In a concordance, look up the words *lie, lies, lying.* Then look up words like *truth* and *honest* or *honesty.* How do you think the number of references to these words corresponds to God's concern in these matters?

2. From one of the verses you found in the listings above, claim one as your own. Write it on the flyleaf of your Bible. Repeat it each day. Ask God to help you be more like him in the area of honesty.

NINE

THE GREENHOUSE OF THE MIND
A Pure Heart

Finding the Heart of Jesus

1. How can you manage your heart "as a greenhouse"? How can you let the analogy get personal?

   A. What kind of "seeds" are you allowing to grow?

   B. What weeds do you see? How can you keep them from flourishing? How do they sometimes crowd out the flowers?

   C. Would you classify yourself as usually optimistic or negative? Explain. How does your optimism or negativism affect those around you?

2. There should be a sentry at the door of our hearts.

   A. Where do your thoughts usually go when you allow them to wander?

B. How can you immediately recognize "wrong thoughts"? How could you do so more easily?

3. We need to submit our thoughts to the authority of Jesus.

    A. If your thoughts were written down on paper and submitted to Christ before you thought them, how many of them would he "red pencil"? Would you be surprised, or would you have known the results beforehand?

    B. If your thoughts were broadcast to those around you, would you be embarrassed? Would they be disappointed? Sad? Hurt? Surprised?

4. The Bible is the "check point" for our questionable thoughts.

    A. In your study of Scripture, what validation can you find for an inferiority complex? A prideful spirit? Conceit? Impure sexual desires?

    B. Some people think the Bible is just a book of no's whose aim is to squelch free-spiritedness. What happens to us when we follow our own "free-spirit" instead of God's Word?

Probing the Mind of Jesus

1. In 1 Peter 5:8–9 the devil is compared to a "roaring lion."

    A. In what circumstances do you most often feel you're going to be "devoured" in your thought life?

B. How can you put up a good resistance to the devil? How can you increase your levels of self-control and alertness?

2. Read Galatians 6:7–10.

A. God recognizes that we become weary in our struggles with sin (v. 9). Once you realize the need to keep your thought life under control (to plant the right seeds), what do you do if you're tempted to give in to spiritual fatigue?

B. What are the benefits that can be reaped from a God-centered thought life?

3. Proverbs 4:20–23 admonishes us to pay close attention to what God says.

A. We are to keep his words not only in our sight but in our hearts. What is the difference between these two?

B. The heart is compared to a "wellspring" of life. Look up the word "wellspring" in a dictionary. Why do you think that word is used in verse 23?

C. You've heard the expression "You are what you eat." Do you believe you are also what you think? Give some examples.

4. In 2 Corinthians 10:3–5 Paul reminds us that though we live in the world, we are not to act as if we are part of the

world (v. 3). He recognizes that life is a fight and reminds us we have been given "divine power" (v. 4) to help win the battle.

A. Verse 5 tells us to "capture" our thoughts, making them obedient to Christ. How can we do this? What are we to do with these thoughts, once we've captured them?

B. How can you tell your wrong, impure, ungodly thoughts no and refuse them readmittance? In what way can this be like a battle?

Becoming the Hands of Jesus

1. Think about a plot of fertile ground for a moment. Is more work involved in the planting stage or the weeding stage? What happens to the crop if the latter is neglected? What market exists for the sale of weeds? Would anyone ever plant weed seeds on purpose? Translate those questions into an evaluation of your thought life. Decide today to plant roses and, with God's help, keep the thistles out.

2. Plant a seed, literally. Use the right soil. Water it. Make sure it gets the correct amount of water and sunshine. Put it where you can see it. Nurture it. Watch it grow. Consider it to be an outward expression of what you are doing inwardly with the garden of your heart.

TEN

FINDING GOLD IN THE GARBAGE
A Hope-Filled Heart

Finding the Heart of Jesus

1. How do you view the "garbage" that comes your way?

   A. Do you think you've had more or less troubles and sorrow than the average person? Explain.

   B. What next "bad thing" are you worried about that might be lurking around the corner?

   C. Why do you think we hang on to the pain and the hurt rather than look for the good in our troubles?

2. How we look at life determines how we live it.

   A. The saying goes "When life gives you lemons, make lemonade." Have you had to make lemonade out of your life circumstances?

   B. Describe someone you know who's good at this. How do you feel when you're around this person? What can you learn from him or her?

3. We need to see our troubles as Jesus sees them.

   A. Analyze your feelings about any unanswered prayers, unfruitful dreams, or unbelievable betrayals. Are they recent, or have you been hanging on to the resulting hurts for a long while? Explain.

B. How can you see these things as Jesus does?

4. Jesus found good in the bad, purpose in the pain.

A. Do you think this is realistically possible in every situation? Explain. What would you say to someone who thought this was a "Pollyanna" view of life?

B. Describe a time you found good in the bad, purpose in the pain. Did you have this attitude while you were going through the difficulty, or did these insights come later? Explain.

5. Jesus can change the way you look at life.

A. How do we often underestimate the power of God?

B. How would your life change if you consistently believed that God's power is the same today as it was in the days of Elisha?

Probing the Mind of Jesus

1. Romans 12:9–16 tells us that troubles are a part of life for everyone; no one is exempt.

A. How should we respond to evil? How are we to behave when afflicted? How is this possible?

B. Why does God allow us to go through these troubles? What do you think is to be gained by them?

C. Do you someday expect to find out God's purpose in your suffering? What if you never do?

2. Compare your spiritual eyesight to that described in Matthew 6:22–23.

   A. Describe someone you know who prefers to live in the darkness rather than the light. Do you enjoy being around this person? Explain.

   B. What's God's opinion about this?

3. Read about Jesus' betrayal in Matthew 26:46–52.

   A. Even after Judas betrayed him, Jesus called him "friend." Have you ever felt betrayed by a "friend." If so, is this person still your friend? Explain.

   B. In so-called righteous indignation, one of Jesus' companions sliced off the ear of the high priest's servant. Luke records that Jesus responded with a healing touch. How can we respond in such a way when we are hurt? What keeps us from responding like this?

4. In Matthew 26:53, Jesus reminds the mob that came for him that he could be rescued from their clutches immediately if he so desired.

   A. In what way can your own difficult situations be easier to handle, knowing that God could get you out of them if he chose to do so? Can they ever be made more difficult because of this knowledge? Explain.

   B. How do you respond when God chooses not to change your circumstances? Do you still believe God is present in the problem? Explain.

Becoming the Hands of Jesus

1. Borrow some eyeglasses from a person with an acute vision problem. Put them up to your eyes. Look at a tree, a flower, the face of the person next to you. Now look at these same objects with your normal vision (with or without glasses). What was the difference? Were things distorted the first time? Were they blurry? It's much easier to see all the detail when you view something in the correct way, isn't it? When viewed through the perfect, all-seeing eyes of God, everything that happens to us makes sense!

2. Think about your friends, especially a friendship that went sour. Did that person hurt you, betray you in a way that still smarts whenever you think of it? Ask the Lord to soften your heart, to forgive him/her. Give your grudge to God and ask him to heal your wounds. Make it a point to pray for your friend by name on a regular basis and look for ways to begin the process of restoration.

ELEVEN

✦◦◦◦✦

WHEN HEAVEN CELEBRATES
A Rejoicing Heart

Finding the Heart of Jesus

1. Jesus knows about the "party"!

A. What is this party? Are you sure you're going to it? How do you know?

B. What did God do to make sure you don't miss the party? What situations did he use? Who were the people involved?

2. Jesus is happiest when the lost are found.

   A. Describe a time when you were separated from your parent, "lost" in a store when you were a child. How did you feel the moment you discovered you were alone? Panic? Fear?

   B. What do you think your parents thought during their search for you? Was there joy when you were found? If so, describe it.

   C. Compare this incident with how God must feel when a sinner repents and comes home to Christ.

3. When you get to the "party," you will be like Jesus. Everyone else will be, too.

   A. Which aspects of Jesus' character do you most desire for yourself?

   B. Which aspects of his character will you appreciate most in others?

   C. How can you love these people right now, while we're all getting ready?

4. Jesus rejoices that we are saved from hell.

A. Describe what you know about hell. Do you believe it's a real place? Why or why not? Read some scriptures that talk about it.

B. How do you rejoice that you're on your way to heaven? Do you ever thank him that you will miss hell? Explain.

5. You can have God's eternal view of the world.

A. Which things that you hold dear to your heart become insignificant when you come to hold God's eternal view of the world?

B. If this viewpoint dominated more of your thinking, how would you spend your time differently?

C. When you hold this view, what happens to your perception of people?

Probing the Mind of Jesus

1. The Psalms are a great place for praise. Read Psalm 96, paying special attention to verses 1 and 2.

A. What does it mean that "all the earth" should sing? Why songs?

B. How and how often do you praise God for your own salvation? How do you respond to other people's salvation stories?

2. Read the three parables of Jesus in Luke 15.

A. Much time and effort was spent in looking for the lost

sheep and the lost coin. What does that say about the lost ones' worth to their owners?

B. Neighbors and friends were called to help rejoice when the lost ones were found. Why was that?

C. The older son in the third story resented the party given for his prodigal brother; he didn't consider his brother worthy of that attention. Do you ever feel someone is "too bad" to be saved, that he/she should not be allowed at the "party" to be held in heaven? Explain. Apart from the grace of God, do you deserve to go?

3. Luke 15:10 speaks of the worth of a single person to God.

A. What should this verse do to our feelings of worthlessness?

B. How should this verse influence your desire to tell others of the salvation that's available in Christ? Does it have this effect with you? Explain.

4. In Matthew 22:13, hell is described as a place "outside," in the dark, where there will be "wailing and gnashing of teeth," with no way out.

A. If this is true, then why do people speak so lightly of that place?

B. Do you think it's important to emphasize the horrors of hell to unbelievers? Explain.

5. Second Corinthians 5:11–16 speaks of a compelling need to tell others of Christ's great gift of salvation.

A. Is it your main purpose in life to bring others to the "party"? How many people have you introduced to Christ so far?

B. Think of someone you know who needs the Lord. How might you be used to introduce this person to Christ? Are you asking God to give you a new heart of love for them? If not, why not?

Becoming the Hands of Jesus

1. Using a concordance or other study tool, search the Scriptures to make a list of all the blessings of heaven. Across the page, write down all the horrors of hell. Then praise God for blessing you with the things in the first list and rescuing you from those in the second.

2. Look through the pages of your favorite hymnal. Find those songs that have to do with heaven. Sing one right now!

TWELVE

FINISHING STRONG
An Enduring Heart

Finding the Heart of Jesus

1. Learn to finish the right things.

A. How much time do you spend on non-essentials?

B. How do you determine what a non-essential is?

2. Finishing strong in the Christian's race takes a massive effort.

   A. At the beginning of your relationship with Christ, were your expectations of the Christian life any different from the reality you have experienced? If so, explain.

   B. Do you think Christians sometimes paint a "too rosy" picture of what life is like after the salvation experience? Describe any examples you can think of.

   C. Would people say you are a stronger believer today than yesterday? Why or why not?

   D. What have been your primary joys as a Christian? Your difficulties?

3. By focusing on the reward ahead, Jesus had the strength to endure the shame of the whole world.

   A. What does it mean to be focused? How focused are you?

   B. What kinds of things most often get in the way of a sharp focus? How can you deal with these more effectively? What keeps you from dealing with them?

4. Jesus looked beyond the horizon, saw the table set before him, and focused on the feast.

   A. If you could have your own feast right now, what would be on the table? Who would be the guests?

B. What do you think that "heavenly feast" will be like?

Probing the Mind of Jesus

1. Spend some time pondering Ephesians 1:15–23.

   A. In verse 18 Paul prays that the eyes of our hearts (our minds) may be "enlightened." Why do you think he says that? What kinds of things have been right in front of you that you still haven't seen?

   B. Describe an inheritance that either you or someone you're close to has received. Try to describe any of the "rich glories" that will be the Christian's inheritance.

   C. How much of God's "incomparably great power" (v. 19) have you experienced? Describe your experiences. What more is left to experience?

2. The Christian race is discussed at length in Hebrews 12.

   A. Why does Paul call the Christian life a "race" instead of a walk, a jog, or some other activity?

   B. What kinds of things hinder you from racing effectively? Do you know anyone who has quit? If so, why did it happen?

   C. How can we continue to joyfully look toward the end? How do we sometimes lose sight of the goal?

   D. Why are you in the race? How can you overcome the urge to stop, rest, and take it easy?

3. The forty-day temptation of Jesus is described in Luke 4:1–13.

A. Jesus ate nothing during this time of temptation and naturally became very hungry. When you are under physical distress, is it harder to keep spiritually focused? Explain. What do you do to compensate?

B. Each time the devil tries to get at Jesus, he responds by using Scripture correctly. How can his example help you in your personal struggles? What strategies can you adopt?

C. The devil attempted to get Christ's eyes off his father, to doubt the love and concern he knew was there. How does Satan use the same tactics with us? How can we respond? How have you responded in the past to such attacks? What happened?

4. Read the parable of the talents in Matthew 25:14–30.

A. With what specific "talents" have you been entrusted? Name them.

B. Do you think the man with five talents had more responsibility than the ones with two or one? Why or why not? If you believe you have just one talent, do you ever spend time wishing God had gifted you with five instead? Explain. How are you using the one you have?

C. Since the one-talent servant knew what his master was like and what he'd expect on his return, why do you suppose he neglected his duty? Do we do this as well? Explain.

D. Compare the master's responses between the more gifted and least gifted servants. In whose place can you most easily put yourself? Why?

E. If you came to the end of your race as a Christian right this minute, would you expect to hear the Master's words as spoken in verse 23? Explain.

Becoming the Hands of Jesus

1. If you are physically able, challenge yourself to a footrace. Set a goal—say, the house at the end of the block—and start running. When you get winded, keep huffing. When you want to quit, don't stop. Make yourself do it. Reward yourself when you get home—try some time alone with a good book. Then make the analogy between your physical exercise and the race we've just been discussing. What do you learn?

2. Take inventory of the projects that surround you, the things that take up the most of your time. Who or what do they benefit? What would happen if you discontinued your involvement? Sort and filter. Resolve to include only those things that prod you on to your goal.

Steps to Peace with God

 Step 1 God's Purpose:
Peace and Life

God loves you and wants you to experience peace and life—abundant and eternal.

The Bible Says . . .

". . . we have peace with God through our Lord Jesus Christ." **Romans 5:1**

"For God so loved the world that He gave His only begotten Son, that whoever believes in Him should not perish but have everlasting life." **John 3:16**

". . . I have come that they may have life, and that they may have it more abundantly." **John 10:10b**

Since God planned for us to have peace and the abundant life right now, why are most people not having this experience?

 Step 2 Our Problem:
Separation

God created us in His own image to have an abundant life. He did not make us as robots to automatically love and obey Him, but gave us a will and a freedom of choice.

We chose to disobey God and go our own willful way. We still make this choice today. This results in separation from God.

Our choice results in separation from God.

The Bible Says . . .

"For all have sinned and fall short of the glory of God." **Romans 3:23**

"For the wages of sin is death, but the gift of God is eternal life in Christ Jesus our Lord." **Romans 6:23**

People (Sinful)   God (Holy)

Our Attempts

There is only one remedy for this problem of separation.

Through the ages, individuals have tried in many ways to bridge this gap . . . without success . . .

The Bible Says . . .

"There is a way that seems right to man, but in the end it leads to death." Proverbs 14:12

"But your iniquities have separated you from God; and your sins have hidden His face from you, so that He will not hear." Isaiah 59:2

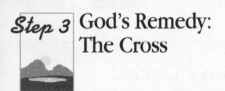

Step 3 God's Remedy: The Cross

Jesus Christ is the only answer to this problem. He died on the Cross and rose from the grave, paying the penalty for our sin and bridging the gap between God and people.

The Bible Says . . .

". . . God is on one side and all the people on the other side, and Christ Jesus, Himself man, is between them to bring them together . . ." 1 Timothy 2:5

"For Christ also has suffered once for sins, the just for the unjust, that He might bring us to God . . ." 1 Peter 3:18a

"But God demonstrates His own love for us in this: While we were still sinners, Christ died for us." Romans 5:8

God has provided the only way . . . we must make the choice . . .

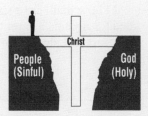

Step 4 | # Our Response: Receive Christ

We must trust Jesus Christ and receive Him by personal invitation.

The Bible Says . . .

"Behold, I stand at the door and knock. If anyone hears My voice and opens the door, I will come in to him and dine with him, and he with Me." Revelation 3:20

"But as many as received Him, to them He gave the right to become children of God, even to those who believe in His name." John 1:12

". . . if you confess with your mouth the Lord Jesus and believe in your heart that God has raised Him from the dead, you will be saved." Romans 10:9

Are you here . . . or here?

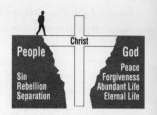

Is there any good reason why you cannot receive Jesus Christ right now?

How to receive Christ:

1. Admit your need (I am a sinner).
2. Be willing to turn from your sins (repent).
3. Believe that Jesus Christ died for you on the Cross and rose from the grave.
4. Through prayer, invite Jesus Christ to come in and control your life through the Holy Spirit. (Receive Him as Lord and Savior.)

What to Pray:

Dear Lord Jesus,

I know that I am a sinner and need Your forgiveness. I believe that You died for my sins. I want to turn from my sins. I now invite You to come into my heart and life. I want to trust and follow You as Lord and Savior.

In Jesus' name. Amen.

_____   _____
Date   Signature

God's Assurance:
His Word

If you prayed this prayer,

The Bible Says...

"For 'whoever calls upon the name of the Lord will be saved.'"
Romans 10:13

Did you sincerely ask Jesus Christ to come into your life? Where is He right now? What has He given you?

"For it is by grace you have been saved, through faith—and this is not from yourselves, it is the gift of God—not by works, so that no one can boast." Ephesians 2:8,9

The
Bible Says...

"He who has the Son has life; he who does not have the Son of God does not have life. These things I have written to you who believe in the name of the Son of God, that you may know that you have eternal life, and that you may continue to believe in the name of the Son of God." 1 John 5:12–13, NKJV

Receiving Christ, we are born into God's family through the supernatural work of the Holy Spirit who indwells every believer...this is called regeneration or the "new birth."

This is just the beginning of a wonderful new life in Christ. To deepen this relationship you should:

1. Read your Bible every day to know Christ better.
2. Talk to God in prayer every day.
3. Tell others about Christ.
4. Worship, fellowship, and serve with other Christians in a church where Christ is preached.
5. As Christ's representative in a needy world, demonstrate your new life by your love and concern for others.

God bless you as you do.

Billy Graham

If you want further help in the decision you have made, write to:
Billy Graham Evangelistic Association P.O. Box 779, Minneapolis, Minnesota 55440-0779

If you are committing your life to Christ, please let us know! We would like to send you Bible study materials and a complimentary six-month subscription to *Decision* magazine to help you grow in your faith.

The Billy Graham Evangelistic Association exists to support the evangelistic ministry and calling of Billy Graham to take the message of Christ to all we can by every prudent means available to us.

Our desire is to introduce as many as we can to the person of Jesus Christ, so that they might experience His love and forgiveness.

Your prayers are the most important way to support us in this ministry. We are grateful for the dedicated prayer support we receive. We are also grateful for those that support us with contributions.

Giving can be a rewarding experience for you and for us at the Billy Graham Evangelistic Association (BGEA). Your gift gives you the satisfaction of supporting an organization that is actively involved in evangelism. Also, it is encouraging to us because part of our ministry is devoted to helping people like you discover and enjoy the stewardship of giving wisely and effectively.

Billy Graham Evangelistic Association
P.O. Box 779
Minneapolis, Minnesota 55440-0779
www.billygraham.org

Billy Graham Evangelistic Association of Canada
P.O. Box 841, Stn Main
Winnipeg, Manitoba R3C 2R3
www.billygraham.ca

Toll free: 1-877-247-2426